GLOB

The

AMSTERDAM

ROBIN GAULDIE

NEW
HOLLAND

First edition published in 2006
by New Holland Publishers (UK) Ltd
London • Cape Town • Sydney • Auckland
10 9 8 7 6 5 4 3 2 1

website: www.newhollandpublishers.com

Garfield House, 86 Edgware Road
London W2 2EA, United Kingdom

80 McKenzie Street
Cape Town 8001, South Africa

14 Aquatic Drive, Frenchs Forest
NSW 2086, Australia

218 Lake Road, Northcote
Auckland, New Zealand

Distributed in the USA by
The Globe Pequot Press, Connecticut

ISBN 1 84537 219 0

Although every effort has been made to ensure
that this guide is up to date and current at time
of going to print, the Publisher accepts no
responsibility or liability for any loss, injury or
inconvenience incurred by readers or travellers
using this guide.

Publishing Manager (UK): Simon Pooley
Publishing Manager (SA): Thea Grobbelaar
DTP Cartographic Manager: Genené Hart
Editor: Thea Grobbelaar
Cover design: Nicole Bannister
Cartographer: Nicole Bannister
Picture Researcher: Shavonne Johannes
Proofreader: Alicha van Reenen

Reproduction by Fairstep (Pty) Ltd, Cape Town
Printed and bound by Times Offset (M) Sdn. Bhd.,
Malaysia.

Photographic Credits:
J Arnold/jonarnoldimages.com: pages 34,
70, 75; **Joe Malone/jonarnold.com:** page 17;
The Bridgeman Art Library: pages 14, 26;
Nigel Hicks: page 84; **International Photo-
bank:** page 19; **International Photobank/
Adrian Baker:** pages 7, 12, 13, 42, 46, 61, 78;
International Photobank/Peter Baker: cover,
pages 6, 20, 41, 44, 45, 48, 63, 65, 74, 79, 80;
Caroline Jones: pages 15, 30, 37; **Life File/
Mike Maidment:** page 83; **Life File/Andrew
Ward:** page 82; **The Mansell Collection:**
pages 8, 10, 11; **Alberto Ramella/
photographersdirect.com:** page 18; **Neil
Setchfield:** title page; **Jeroen Snijders:** pages
16, 21, 22, 24, 25, 27, 28, 29, 32, 33, 35, 36,
39, 40, 43, 47, 49, 50, 51, 52, 53, 54, 60, 62,
66, 68, 69, 72, 73, 81; **RichardWareham/
photographersdirect.com:** page 23;
www.amsterdam.info: page 31.

Front Cover: Built in 1512, the Montelbaanstoren was part of the city's defences.
Title Page: The Singel, the oldest and inner-
most of Amsterdam's canal rings.

CONTENTS

⊕ **USING THIS BOOK**   **4**

🅟 **OVERVIEW**   **6**
The Land   6
History in Brief   8
Government & Economy   12
The People   13

⊕ **HIGHLIGHTS**   **14**
Rijksmuseum   14
Rijksmuseum Vincent
   van Gogh   16
Koninklijk Paleis   17
Stedelijk Museum   18
Amsterdams Historisch
   Museum   19
Begijnhof   20
Oude Kerk   21
Het Rembrandthuis   22
Joods Historisch Museum   23
Hortus Botanicus
   Amsterdam   24
Anne Frank Huis   25
Six Collection   26
Willet Holthuysen
   Museum   27
Westerkerk   28
Scheepvaart Museum   29
Nieuwe Kerk   30
Museum Amstelkring   31
Albert Cuypstraat
   Market   32
Heineken Brewery
   Museum   33

🅞 **SIGHTSEEING**   **34**
Places of Worship   34
Museums   35
Green Spaces   39

🅥 **ACTIVITIES**   **41**
Sport and Recreation   41

Alternative Amsterdam   42
Walking Tours   44
Organized Tours   46
Fun for Children   47

🅢 **SHOPPING**   **50**
Shops   51
Markets   51

🅐 **ACCOMMODATION**   **54**
Where to Stay   54
Hotels   55

🅞 **EATING OUT**   **60**
Food and Drink   60
Where to Eat   63
Restaurants   64

🅔 **ENTERTAINMENT**   **70**
Nightlife   70
Cinema   70
Theatre   71
Internet Cafés   71
Conference Centre   72
Classical Music and Opera   72
Rock, Jazz and Blues   74
Striptease   75
Gay and Lesbian Clubs   76
Discos and Dance Clubs   76

🅔 **EXCURSIONS**   **78**
The Hague   78
Delft   79
Rotterdam   80
Leiden   81
Haarlem and Utrecht   82
Gouda   83

🅐 **TRAVEL TIPS**   **84**

INDEX OF SIGHTS   **92**
GENERAL INDEX   **93**

MAKE THE MOST OF YOUR GUIDE

Reading these two pages will help you to get the most out of your guide and save you time when using it. Sites discussed in the text are cross-referenced with the cover maps – for example, the reference 'Map A–C3' refers to the Central Amsterdam map (Map A), column C, row 3. Use the Map Plan below to quickly locate the map you need.

MAP PLAN

Outside Back Cover   Outside Front Cover

Inside Front Cover   Inside Back Cover

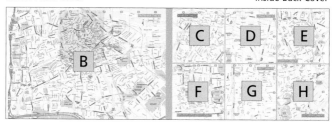

THE BIGGER PICTURE

Key to Map Plan

A – Central Amsterdam
B – Amsterdam
C – Haarlem
D – Leiden
E – Utrecht
F – Den Haag (The Hague)
G – Delft
H – Rotterdam
I – Excursions
J – Gouda

Key to Symbols

⊠ — address

☎ — telephone

🖋 — fax

🖳 — website

🖰 — e-mail address

🕘 — opening times

🚌 — transport

💰 — entry fee

🍴 — restaurants nearby

M — nearest metro station

Map Legend

motorway		main road	**Spuistraat**
national road		other road	Leliegracht
main road		mall	NIEUWENDIJK
minor road		built-up area	
metro	Centraal Ⓜ	one-way arrow	←
tram		shopping centre	Ⓢ Magna Plaza
bus route			
railway		sqaure	Nieuw Markt
river		route number	E19
route number	E19	parking area	🅿
city	LEIDEN	building of interest	Amstelhof
major town	⊙ Delft	library	📖
town	O Edam	post office	⊠
large village	◎ Zevenhoven	tourist information	ⓘ
village	O Zaanse Schans		
airport	✈ ✈	place of worship	△
place of interest	• Boerenmarkt	police station	●
viewpoint	📷	bus terminus	🚍
golf course	⛳		
hotel	Ⓗ VICTORIA	hospital	⊕
park & garden	Vondelpark		

Keep us Current

Travel information is apt to change, which is why we regularly update our guides. We'd be most grateful to receive feedback from you if you've noted something we should include in our updates. If you have any new information, please share it with us by writing to the Publishing Manager, Globetrotter, at the office nearest to you (addresses on the imprint page of this guide). The most significant contribution to each new edition will be rewarded with a free copy of the updated guide.

Above: *A canal cruise is one of the best ways to see Amsterdam.*

AMSTERDAM

Amsterdam is a city where the land meets the sea, old meets new, and bohemian lifestyles rub shoulders with hard-headed commercialism and bourgeois respectability. A rich cultural heritage combines with a lively dynamism to make this small but cosmopolitan capital one of the most popular European destinations every year, drawing millions of visitors from all over the world.

It is a city of rich variety, from the gentrified **Jordaan** district to the bustling city centre and the narrow streets of the **Old Side**, where medieval churches look down on the gaudy neon of the raffish **red light district**. It can also boast picturesque old canalside homes, houseboats, tulip-filled parks, tree-lined waterways and superb museums unmatched in Europe.

The Land

Amsterdam stands on the estuary of the River **IJ**, close to its mouth on the landlocked **IJsselmeer** and about 20km (12½ miles) from the North Sea coast. Until the 1950s, IJsselmeer, then known as the Zuider Zee, was an open bight of the North Sea; it was dammed to allow land reclamation and its taming is one of the great triumphs for the Dutch in their battle with the sea.

With the introduction of steam-powered pumps in the 19th century the tide finally turned in favour of the city and the last inland seas – such as the Harlemmermeer, where Amsterdam Schiphol Airport now stands – were drained to create reclaimed farmlands called polders.

City Profile

The river IJ separates central Amsterdam from the residential suburbs on the north shore. Along the south bank of the IJ are the city's docklands. Concentric, semicircular rings of canals spread south from the IJ, dividing central Amsterdam from an outer crescent of mainly residential suburbs. Further south and west are Amsterdam's industrial and commercial areas.

Amsterdam's historic heart is enclosed by the canals that link the **River Amstel** with the IJ. The oldest part of the city is enclosed by the ring of the **Singel** canal on the south and west and by the **Kloveniers Burgwal** canal on the east. Beyond the centre are newer canal rings: the **Herengracht**, **Keizersgracht** and **Prinsengracht**, built during the city's 17th-century Golden Age.

The canals, originally built to drain marshy land, have become Amsterdam's major feature. Building land has always been in short supply, so houses are squeezed side by side along the canals. Buildings are narrow, five or six storeys high, and set on a foundation of piles driven through the soft surface to firmer ground below. Many older buildings lean drunkenly against their neighbours as their foundations subside with time. In summer, apartment dwellers make up for the lack of a garden with window boxes full of flowers.

Climate
Amsterdam has a northern European climate. **Summer** (Jun–Sep) can be warm, but cool and rainy weather is always a possibility. **Autumn** is a cool and misty season, giving way in October to increasingly cold, wet and windy weather. The nearby North Sea always makes its presence felt, and sub-zero **winter** temperatures in the centre are not all that uncommon. Winter is rarely far off freezing point, and the canals when frozen and snow-covered are every bit as pretty as in spring and summer. **Spring** (Apr–May) is one of the most popular times to visit Amsterdam and the Netherlands, with the trees along the canals springing into new leaf and the famous bulb fields in brilliant bloom.

Below: *Bulb fields colour the countryside in spring.*

OVERVIEW

Canal Bird Life
There is little wildlife to be seen in central Amsterdam, where the closely packed streets and buildings and sparse greenery leave little room even for hardy urban survivors like pigeons and sparrows. Along the canals, though, it is a different matter. Look out in spring and early summer for coots, dabchicks, great crested grebes and mallard, all of which build messy floating nests on buoys, mooring platforms and niches along the canalside.

Below: *The Dutch were actively involved in sea trade.*

History in Brief

In prehistoric and Roman times, and into the early Middle Ages, the site on which Amsterdam now stands was marshland between the North Sea and the estuaries of the IJ and Amstel rivers. Later it became a small fishing settlement, but by the early 13th century the original village of **Aemstelle Dam** – the dam on the Amstel – had grown into a prosperous small town.

The sea gave Amsterdam a highway to ports all over Europe and the rivers carried its trade goods far inland. Through the Middle Ages Amsterdam's prosperity was boosted by commerce, first with other North Sea ports, then with the powerful Hanseatic League of Baltic trading cities, and eventually even further afield. In 1489 Emperor Maximilian I granted Amsterdam the royal seal and his personal protection. The city was one of the wealthiest and most important in 15th-century Europe.

Reformation

During the Reformation, the radical ideas of Martin Luther, Erasmus and Calvin were quickly taken up by the Dutch and the Netherlands became a refuge for Protestants from less liberal parts of the continent. In 1522 Emperor Charles V introduced the **Inquisition** to quell the forces of the Reformation and restore Catholic orthodoxy. In the next 30 years 30,000 people were executed for their

History in Brief

Protestant beliefs, but the Inquisition still failed to bring the Netherlands back into the Catholic fold.

The Struggle for Independence

Dissidence turned into armed resistance in 1568, following the brutal occupation of Amsterdam by the Spanish **Duke of Alva**. The rebels were no match for Alva's seasoned veterans in the field, but under **Prince William of Orange** ('William the Silent') they fought a guerrilla campaign by land and sea.

In 1581 the united northern provinces of the Netherlands renounced allegiance to Spain, declaring themselves a republic ruled by the **States General**, made up of a representative of each of the seven provinces (advocates) and the Stadhouder, William (the Silent) of Orange. William was assassinated by a Catholic fanatic on 10 July 1584, but although hostilities with Spain were to continue intermittently for the next 80 years, Dutch independence was firmly established.

The Golden Age

Amsterdam's tolerance attracted refugees from all over Europe, bringing with them new skills, trade contacts and investment. The city became a haven for painters such as **Rembrandt** and **Vermeer** and the philosophers **Spinoza**, **Descartes** and **Lipsius**. Religious tolerance was also extended to those Dutch Catholics who chose not to renounce their faith.

By the mid-17th century work began on the Herengracht, Keizersgracht and Prinsengracht. Merchants built luxurious townhouses along the new canals and their wealth trickled down to painters and craftsmen.

Unspoken Hero
William the Silent, Prince of the House of Orange and the first Stadhouder of the free Netherlands, earned his nickname by his reluctance to come out for the Protestant cause until 1568, when he led the first campaign against the Spanish Duke of Alva, beginning the Eighty Years War against Spain. Ten years later his rebel army and fleet had driven the Spaniards out of the Netherlands – Amsterdam was the last city to surrender to him – and he was chosen by the States General (the governing council) to be the newly independent country's first Stadhouder.

Above: *In the mid-17th century the Dutch Fleet ruled from the North Sea to the Indian Ocean.*
Opposite: *Louis Bonaparte, ill-fated king of the Netherlands.*

Eastern Adventure

In 1595 **Cornelis de Houtman** launched an expedition to break the Spanish-Portuguese monopoly of the trade routes to the East Indies. In 1602 the merchants formed the **United East India Company** (Vereinigde Oost-indische Compagnie) to protect their Asian enterprise. Overseas, the wealthy and influential VOC was in effect the Dutch government, with the rights of a sovereign power.

Meanwhile, the less successful **West India Company** carried Dutch colours west to the Caribbean and the Americas. However, much of the wealth of the West India Company came from slave trafficking between West Africa and the Caribbean.

Revolution, Invasion and Monarchy

Wars with England and France followed in the 17th and 18th centuries, but the Dutch held their own surprisingly well considering the might of their opponents.

In 1688, with the overthrow of King James II of England, Stadhouder **William III**, husband of James's daughter Mary, was invited to take the British throne. Alliance with England involved the Netherlands in wars with France from 1688–97, the War of Spanish Succession (1702–13) and the Seven Years War (1756–63). The Golden Age drew to a close. Amsterdam remained prosperous, becoming one of Europe's most important financial centres and generating almost a quarter of the Republic's entire income.

HISTORY IN BRIEF

At the end of the 18th century, French Emperor **Napoleon Bonaparte** set up his brother, **Louis,** as King of the Netherlands, but in 1813 the Stadhouder William V returned to make himself King William I over an expanded Netherlands. The new kingdom included the southern provinces (now Belgium) for the first time; in 1831–2 the southern provinces rose in revolt and Belgium became an independent kingdom.

Occupation and Liberation

During **World War I** the Netherlands remained neutral, but this was not an option during **World War II**. In May 1940 Germany invaded. By early 1941 the occupiers had begun rounding up Amsterdam's Jewish citizens for transportation to concentration camps in Germany and Poland. Allied troops liberated the Netherlands in May 1945, arriving in Amsterdam only a few days before the end of the war.

Modern Amsterdam

Amsterdam's traditional tolerance of different faiths finds expression in a modern-day liberalism which some believe has gone too far. A relaxed approach to pornography means hard-core porn is openly on display next to more innocuous picture postcards. Legalization of prostitution has given the city one of Europe's most lurid red-light districts. The city has become a gay magnet. Decriminalizing soft drug use has also made the city the cannabis capital of Europe. Amsterdam has become a cosmopolitan city, and immigrants account for about 30% of its population.

> **The 19th Century**
> Through the early 19th century Amsterdam and the Netherlands became a backwater, and only in the latter part of the century was the economy revitalized. The age of steam made Amsterdam a vital link between Europe's railway networks and transatlantic services, while wealth poured into the city from the South African diamond mines. It was almost a second Golden Age; many of Amsterdam's public buildings, including the Rijksmuseum, Centraal Station, the Beurs and others, date from this era. Overseas, the Dutch continued to expand their empire in the East Indies, bringing most of what is now Indonesia under their control. In the 1870s, the VOC's monopoly was ended and private investment in the colonies was allowed, opening up a new flow of trade.

Below: *The Binnen-
hof in The Hague,
seat of the first
Dutch parliament.*

Government and Economy

The Netherlands is a constitutional monarchy. The House of Orange, the dynasty
founded by William the Silent, remains on
the throne in the person of **Queen Beatrix**,
who succeeded her mother, Queen Juliana,
in 1980. The Dutch have a deep affection
for their royal family, but the monarchy
has no real political power. Executive and
legislative power is in the hands of an
elected prime minister and a two-chamber
parliament which meets in **The Hague**.
Amsterdam is governed by a mayor and
city council.

The Netherlands was a founding member of the **European Union** and was among
the first to adopt the common European
currency, the Euro, but in 2005 a solid
majority voted against the adoption of a
common EU constitution – a vote that
reflected growing disenchantment with
the European Union.

Amsterdam is a major **commercial** and
financial centre. **Tourism** is also one of the

city's bigger moneyspinners,
with over 3 million foreign visitors annually. The administra-
tive and service sectors, along
with tourism, are the city's
major employers. Rotterdam's
vast Europoort complex is
Europe's biggest seaport, both
in area and in terms of tonnage
handled, but Amsterdam is also
a busy **shipping** centre.

Standards of living are high,
with the Netherlands ranking as
one of the most prosperous
European nations.

The People

Amsterdam welcomed refugee Protestants and Jews in the 15th and 16th centuries, hid Jews from the Nazis, and accepted waves of immigrants from developing countries in the latter half of the 20th century. But there are worrying signs of a backlash against the long-standing liberal consensus, following the murders by Islamic extremists of anti-immigration politician Pim Fortuyn and film-maker Theo van Gogh – both of whom were seen as anti-Muslim.

Above: *Amsterdammers enjoying the sunshine at one of the city's many outdoor cafés.*

The Netherlands has always been quick to dispense with governments which ignore the will of the people. Since the mid-1990s the national government has been left of centre, but Amsterdam's politics tend to be more liberal than those of the country as a whole, with left-wingers controlling the city council even when centre- right national governments are in power.

In the 1980s and 90s there was considerable sympathy for the squatters' movement, which had grown out of youth protest and played a part in resisting the conversion of central Amsterdam from a living and working community into a sterile commercial district.

Women occupy a high proportion of seats in the Dutch parliament and on the Amsterdam city council and enjoy legal protection against exploitation at home and at work.

In 2001 the city council met acclaim from liberals and protest from conservatives when it voted to put homosexual relationships on the same legal basis as conventional marriages. Also in 2001, Holland became the first country in Europe to legalize euthanasia.

Language

Dutch is closely related to German. Grammar and vocabulary are not hard for English-speakers to grasp, but the Dutch often find amusement in foreigners' attempts to come to terms with the idiosyncratic vowels and consonants of their language. Learning how to pronounce place names can be tricky. Few visitors realize that IJ and Spui both rhyme with 'eye'. Other sounds are easier. The double 'a' (as in *centraal* and *nationaal*) is pronounced just as it looks. Attempts to master a few basic phrases will always be appreciated, and a grasp of place name pronunciation will certainly help you to find your way around.

Rijksmuseum
✉ Stadhouderskade 42
☎ 020 674 7000, or
020 673 2121
📠 020 674 7001
📧 info@
rijksmuseum.nl
🖥 www.
rijksmuseum.nl
🕐 10:00–18:00 daily
💰 9 Euros
🚋 Tram 2, 5, 6, 7, 10
🍴 Café-restaurant

See Map B–D3 ★ ★ ★

RIJKSMUSEUM

The Rijksmuseum has more than 5000 paintings, a million prints and drawings, and thousands of sculptures. A detailed guide to the museum's displays is available from the information desk in the first-floor foyer.

The jewels of the Rijksmuseum collection are on the first floor, where room after room traces the course of Dutch painting from the stiff religious art of the early medieval era to the increasingly easy and fluid styles of the Renaissance and Golden Age of the 16th and 17th centuries.

Opposite: *The Rijksmuseum, a treasury of great art.*
Below: *Tintoretto's beautiful Otavia Strada, one of the many fabulous artworks on display at the Rijksmuseum.*

Paintings are exhibited more or less in chronological order, putting the works of masters such as **Frans Hals**, **Jacob van Ruisdael** and **Jan Vermeer** into the context of their times. Essential viewing includes the series of panels by the **Master of Alkmaar**, *The Seven Works of Charity*, dating from 1504, in Room 204; two perfect landscapes

by **Jan Brueghel the Elder** – neither of them bigger than 15x23cm (6x9in) – in Room 207, a tiny circular annex whose walls are covered with delightful miniatures; and the lively portrait of the cheerfully dishevelled *Merry Drinker* by Frans Hals, whose works dominate Rooms 208–210.

Worth looking out for in Rooms 215 and 216 are portraits by **Jan Steen** of himself and his family, which are full of charm and mark a departure by Dutch painters from their staid tableaux of the wealthy and powerful. Landscapes and townscapes adorn Rooms 217–221, and Room 221A contains four perfect small paintings by **Jan Vermeer**: *The Milkmaid*, *The Little Street*, *Woman Reading a Letter* and *The Love Letter*.

The superb **Rembrandt Collection** is also on this floor. In Room 211 his early work is usually on display with paintings by earlier masters who influenced him, such as **Pieter Lastman**. Neighbouring rooms are filled with monumental landscapes and detailed representations from Classical and Biblical mythology.

Rembrandt's best-known work, usually called *The Night Watch*, is in Room 224. Room 223 displays background material about the picture, including evidence that when painted it was even bigger; 30cm (12in) were trimmed from the top and 60cm (2ft) from the left-hand side in the early 18th century, apparently to make it fit into the space allocated for it in the Stadhuys on the Dam (now the Royal Palace, *see* page 17).

Between Room 224 and the foyer is the **Gallery of Honour**, where pride of place is usually given to other Rembrandt masterpieces and works by other painters of the Rembrandt school. Rembrandt's *The Jewish Bride* and *The Syndics*, both painted towards the end of his life, are usually in Room 229 and 230. Other painters often on display here include **Ferdinand Bol**, **Govert Flinck** and **Aert de Gelder**, all followers of Rembrandt.

The Night Watch
The true name of this most famous of Rembrandt's paintings is in fact *The Guard Company of Captain Frans Banning Cocq and Lieutenant Willem van Ruijtenburch*. Recent restoration revealed that the painting's colours have been darkened by time and dirt and that the 'Night Watch' are actually shown emerging into bright sunlight from the dark shadows of a city gateway. Portraits of guard companies like these were routinely commissioned by the commanders of Amsterdam's civic militia, but Rembrandt's painting is unusual in its depiction of vigour and action. Paintings of the same subject by other artists, also on display in the museum, show guard companies drawn up stiffly on parade.

See Map B–D4   ★ ★ ★

Above: *The superb Rijksmuseum Vincent van Gogh.*

RIJKSMUSEUM VINCENT VAN GOGH

This museum is one of the city's most popular sights. It has the world's biggest and most varied collection of Van Gogh's work, including 200 paintings and 500 drawings. These are complemented by a fine collection of work by his contemporaries, including **Gauguin**, **Monet** and **Toulouse-Lautrec**. Exhibits also include Van Gogh's collection of engravings and Japanese prints and his letters to his brother Theo. The museum has a rotating exhibition on the ground floor providing an introduction to the painter's life and work.

The main permanent collection of Van Gogh's work hangs on the first floor. In the two years before his death at age 37 in 1890, he painted over 200 works, from the earthy *Potato Eaters*, redolent of northern European farm life, to the almost hallucinogenic radiance of the *Sunflowers* of southern France. The paintings are grouped by theme, illustrating how Van Gogh's treatment of the same subject might change almost from day to day. Also on the first floor, the **Print Room** gives some clues to Van Gogh's earlier influences, notably the Japanese printmakers Kesai and Hiroshige. In 1999 a dramatic new exhibition wing designed by Kisho Kurokawa opened. It is used for temporary exhibitions of art and architecture.

Rijksmuseum Vincent van Gogh
✉ Paulus Potterstraat 7
☎ 020 570 5200
📠 020 570 5222
✆ info@vangogh
museum.nl
🖥 www.vangogh
museum.nl
🕐 10:00–18:00 daily
💰 10 Euros
🚋 Tram 2, 5
🍽 Restaurant

Van Gogh Museum & Royal Palace

See Map A–D3 ★ ★ ★

KONINKLIJK PALEIS

The Royal Palace was built between 1648 and 1655 at the height of the Golden Age. The Baroque-Classical façade is crowned by an elaborately carved pediment decorated with unicorns and other allegorical creatures. On the roof are statues of the Virtues, and looking down from the back is Atlas, bearing a globe. The huge cupola is crowned by a weathervane in the shape of a galleon.

The great halls are lavishly furnished. On the ground floor, biblical allegories in stone decorate the **Marble Tribunal**, once the city's main courtroom; condemned prisoners were taken from here to be hanged on a public scaffold on the Dam. Each upper floor room housed a different department of the city administration and is adorned with works of art appropriate to their function.

Most impressive is the grand **Burgerzaal** (Citizens' Hall). Louis Bonaparte used it as his throne room: its interior is clad almost entirely in marble and its floor is inlaid with maps of the world. The galleries surrounding the hall display dynamic canvases of early Dutch history by Jan Lievens, Govert Flinck, Jacob Jordaens and Juriaan Ovens.

Before leaving the palace, visit the 10-minute slide show on historic Amsterdam and check out the relief map of the medieval city on the ground floor.

Koninklijk Paleis
✉ Nieuwezijds Voorburgwal 147
☎ 020 620 4060
📠 020 623 3819
✆ info@kon-paleis amsterdam.nl
🖥 www.koninklijkhuis.nl
💰 4.50 Euros
🚊 Tram 4, 9, 14, 16, 24, 25

Below: *The Royal Palace is the most imposing historic building in the Netherlands.*

Stedelijk Museum
✉ Oosterdokkade 5
☎ 020 572 2911
📠 020 675 2716
🖐 info@stedelijk.nl
🖥 www.stedelijk.nl
🕐 11:00–17:00 daily
(Oct–Mar), 11:00–
19:00 (Apr–Sep)
💰 8 Euros
🚋 Tram 1, 2, 4, 5, 9,
13, 16, 17, 24, 25
M Centraal
🍽 restaurants in
Centraal Station

See Map B–D4   ★★★

STEDELIJK MUSEUM

This museum is temporarily housed at Oosterdok (near Centraal Station) while its main
premises at the Museumplein are renovated.
Its innovative exhibitions are always chal-
lenging, and it is regarded as one of the
world's leading museums of modern art,
with a collection that includes works by
Monet, **Cezanne** and **Picasso**.

The rotating collection of works from the
permanent collection usually includes some
lovely Cezanne landscapes, at least one of
the handful of Van Goghs left behind when
the Van Gogh collection moved to its own
museum, and works by Matisse, Chagall and
Kandinsky. The Stedelijk's real highlight is its
outstanding portfolio of works by **pop
artists** of the 1960s, such as Andy Warhol
and Roy Lichtenstein, and its collection of
works by **living artists** – including members
of the COBRA (COpenhagen-BRussels-Ams-
terdam) movement – is quite an eye-opener.

Among the most striking exhibits are the
unqiue works by the Russian abstract
painter Kazimir Malevich and the Dutch
painters of the De Stijl movement, Piet
Mondriaan and Theo van Doesberg. The
Stedelijk is also noted for its print collection,
which is displayed separately and includes
an ever-changing
and eclectic array
of work by living
photographers as
well as the poster
artists and print-
makers from ear-
lier decades.

Below: *One of the
world's leading
modern art
museums, the
Stedelijk Museum.*

See Map A–D4 ★★★

AMSTERDAMS HISTORISCH MUSEUM

Housed in one of the city's oldest buildings, the former municipal orphanage was converted into a museum in 1975. The museum is a vivid combination of modern displays and older memorabilia, intelligently laid out in 20 exhibition rooms. All 20 rooms merit a visit, but if time is limited you should certainly not miss the museum's high points. First, climb the spiral stair to the **Bell Room**, where 17th-century bells from the Munttoren are on display and recorded chimes from the Royal Palace and the city's three great churches can be heard.

Above: *The Amsterdam Historical Museum houses a fascinating collection.*

The paths taken by Amsterdam's merchant adventurers are shown in lights on a large **map** in another room – a graphic example of the extent of the city's 16th- and 17th-century trading empire, which spanned the entire known world and was at the cutting edge of exploration.

In the museum's **restaurant**, David and Goliath, you will see Goliath himself, in the shape of a gigantic armoured statue. Next to him stands a tiny, life-sized David. Between 1650 and 1680 the giant stood in the city's amusement park; his eyes could roll and his head could move – pretty sophisticated stuff for the 17th century.

The **Schuttergalerij** (Guards' Gallery) is a covered street lined with group portraits of militia companies. Rembrandt and Frans Hals among others were commissioned to portray the watch companies of their day. The portraits here are by less famous artists.

Amsterdams Historisch Museum
✉ Kalverstraat 92
☎ 020 523 1822
📠 020 620 7789
📧 info@ahm.nl
🖥 www.ahm.nl
🕐 10:00–17:00 Mon–Fri, 11:00–17:00 weekends
💰 6 Euros
🚋 Tram 1, 2, 4, 5, 9, 11, 14, 16, 24, 25
🍴 David and Goliath, ground floor of the museum

⊙ See Map A–C4 ★★★

Above: *Elaborately decorated gables surrounding the Begijnhof.*

BEGIJNHOF

The Begijnhof is a court-yard of lovely buildings surrounding a green. Among them, at No. 34, is the oldest house in Amsterdam. This is the last surviving wooden house in the city, dating from the 15th century. After several devastating conflagrations, the municipality banned all-wood buildings in 1521. Above the door of No. 34 is the legend *Het Wouten Huys*: The Wooden House.

In front of it is a charming monument to the **Beguines** or Begijns, the order of lay sisters who founded their community here in 1346. They rejected the cloistered life of the nunnery – each sister had her own small house and was not subject to the rule of a Mother Superior – but devoted their lives to helping the ill and the poor.

In the centre of the square is the original **Begijnkerk** chapel, built in 1419. The Begijns were deprived of their church during the Reformation in 1578; in 1607 it was taken over by Presbyterian refugees from England, and is still known as the **English Church**. It has the only unaltered medieval church tower in the city. Like other Catholics in the post-Reformation Netherlands, the Begijns had to worship clandestinely; their 'secret' church, next to Het Wouten Huys, is still in use. The last of the Begijns, Sister Antonia, died in 1971, and the pretty apartments surrounding the square now house elderly widows.

Handy Hoists

At first glance, any one of the city's canalside houses can look much like the next. However, the buildings are embellished with elaborate gables and distinctive decorative gablestones. Protruding from many gables is a solid wooden beam, still used to hoist furniture from street- or canal-level through upper storey windows, as stairways are far too narrow to accommodate pianos, wardrobes or dining-room tables.

⭐ See Map A–E2   ★ ★ ★

OUDE KERK

The Oude Kerk (Old Church), situated on the west side of Oudezijds Voorburgwal, overlooks the Old Side and is the oldest church in Amsterdam. Archaeological work done here indicates that a small church existed on this canal-side site as early as the 13th century. The Gothic church tower dates from 1306, but most of the rest of this solid, seemingly massive brick building, dwarfing the houses which surround it, was added or rebuilt in the 16th century. The 65m (210ft) wooden steeple was added in 1566 and the interior has been altered many times over almost seven centuries.

The splendid altars the Oude Kerk had during the Roman Catholic era were destroyed during the Reformation, when the church became a Protestant place of worship, but three of the lovely stained-glass windows survive from 1555 in the Chapel of Our Lady. Designed by the artist Pieter Aert-zoon (c1508–1579), these glowing works of religious art show scenes from the Nativity and the Annunciation.

Among those who are buried in the Oude Kerk is Rembrandt van Rijn's wife, Saskia, whose tomb is on the north side of the church.

Oude Kerk
✉ Oudekerksplein 23
☎ 020 625 8284
📠 info@oudekerk.nl
🖥 www.oudekerk.nl
🕐 11:00–17:00 Mon–Sat, 13:00–17:00 Sun
💰 3.80 Euros
🚊 Tram 4, 9, 16, 24, 25

Below: *The Oude Kerk, as its name suggests, is the oldest church in Amsterdam.*

Het Rembrandthuis
✉ Jodenbreestraat 4–6
☎ 020 520 0400
📠 020 520 0401
📧 museum@
rembrandthuis.nl
💻 www.rembrandt
huis.nl
🕓 10:00–17:00 Mon–
Sat, 13:00–17:00 Sun
💰 7 Euros
🚋 Tram 9, 14
Ⓜ Waterlooplein

◎ *See Map A–F4* | ★ ★ ★

HET REMBRANDTHUIS

Rembrandt bought the town house with red shutters at Jodenbreestraat 4–6, close to the St Antonies Sluis, in 1639. He lived here for almost 20 years, until he was declared bankrupt in 1658 and the house was sold. The building is now a museum, with 250 of Rembrandt's etchings on show. All are worth looking at, but there are too many to take in at once.

The house also contains a recreation of Rembrandt's 'cabinet of curiosities'. Like many artists and intellectuals of his time, the painter was a keen collector of antiques and objects and artefacts from the new frontiers of Asia, Africa and the Americas, all of which were being opened up by Dutch merchant adventurers. Fossils, weapons, costumes and stuffed animals

Opposite: *The Jewish History Museum in the restored synagogue.*
Below: *Rembrandt's former home now houses a collection of his etchings.*

form a glorious clutter in a room similar to the one Rembrandt would have used for inspiration for his paintings and etchings. The house was converted into a museum in 1896 and marked the fourth centenary of Rembrandt's birth with a series of landmark exhibitions in 2006, with many of the artist's works returning to the place where they were originally created for the first time in 400 years.

See Map A–F5   ★★★

JOODS HISTORISCH MUSEUM

The Jewish Historical Museum is housed in a complex of four former synagogues whose interiors have been painstakingly reconstructed. The oldest, the **Great Synagogue**, was built in 1671 and was the first synagogue built in western Europe. The opening of the Great Synagogue was followed by the building of the **Obbene Shul** (Upstairs Synagogue) in 1685, the **Dritt Shul** (Third Synagogue) 15 years later and the **Neie Shul** (New Synagogue) in 1752.

A collection of religious objects displayed here includes the marvellous marble ark of the Great Synagogue, some elaborate silverware, gorgeously embroidered prayer shawls and exhibitions of the work of Dutch Jewish painters.

An exhibition also highlights the the role of Jews in the development of Amsterdam's trade and industry. A grimmer note is struck by the exhibition downstairs, showing false identification papers and ration cards Jewish people used in the struggle to evade capture by the Nazis.

Located in Mr Visserplein, the **Portuguese Synagogue** was built in 1675 and survived World War II. It was restored in the 1950s. Its interior, with a lofty, barrel-vaulted roof, was intended by its architect, Elias Bouman, to echo that of the Temple of Solomon as described in the Bible. The huge space is lit by scores of arched windows and original 17th-century brass chandeliers.

Joods Historisch Museum
✉ Nieuwe Amstelstraat 1
☎ 020 626 9945
🖷 020 624 1721
✆ info@jhm.nl
💻 www.jhm.nl
🕔 11:00–17:00 daily, except Yom Kippur
💰 6.50 Euros
🚊 Tram 9
Ⓜ Waterlooplein
🍴 Kosher restaurant

Portuguese Synagogue
✉ Mr Visserplein 3
☎ 020 624 5351
🖷 020 625 4680
✆ m.dori@esnoga.com
💻 www.esnoga.com
🕔 11:00–16:00 Sun–Fri, closed Sat and Jewish holidays
💰 6.50 Euros
🚊 Tram 9
Ⓜ Waterlooplein

See Map B–F3 ★★★

Above: *Greenhouses at the Hortus Botanicus shelter plants from every continent.*

Hortus Botanicus Amsterdam
✉ Plantage Midden-laan 2A
☎ 020 625 9021
📠 020 625 7026
📧 info@dehortus.nl
🖥 www.dehortus.nl
🕓 09:00–17:00 Mon–Fri, 11:00–17:00 Sat–Sun (Apr–Sep); 09:00–16:00 Mon–Fri, 11:00–16:00 Sat–Sun (Oct–Mar)
💰 6 Euros
🚊 Tram 9, 14
Ⓜ Waterlooplein
🍴 Orangery outdoor café-restaurant

HORTUS BOTANICUS AMSTERDAM

The Botanical Garden was laid out in 1682, its purpose primarily scientific and commercial. Here, Amsterdam's doctors and apothecaries grew and studied medicinal herbs, spices and other plants brought back by Dutch explorers from Asia, Africa and the Americas. One of the garden's main sponsors was the Dutch East India Company, which was keen to find new ways of keeping seamen in good health on long voyages. The horticulturalists also studied new crops and potentially profitable plants – such as coffee, cinnamon, oil palm and pineapple – from Dutch possessions overseas. The first coffee in South America came from seeds grown here. These seeds were obtained from plants brought by Dutch sailors from the East.

The gardens boast more than 4000 kinds of plant, and include a medicinal herb garden, an orangery, a monumental palm house and sophisticated tropical greenhouses. In spring there is a superb array of tulips. The Dutch obsession with tulips dates from the mid-16th century, when they were first brought here from Turkey, and the Hortus Botanicus has an annual array of some of the most dazzlingly colourful varieties that Dutch tulip-growers have created over the past four centuries – including the deep purple 'Black Parrot', the nearest approach to the legendary black tulip yet developed.

⊙ *See* Map A–B2 | ★ ★ ★

ANNE FRANK HUIS

The house at No. 263 was made famous by the diary kept by Anne Frank, who hid with her Jewish family from the Nazis in a secret apartment above her father's herb and spice warehouse. The Franks, the Van Daan family and a dentist named Dussel stayed hidden from July 1942 until August 1944, when they were betrayed to the Germans. Anne's father was the only one to survive the German concentration camps. The diary was found by an office cleaner and published in 1947.

The crowds of visitors make a visit to the tiny, empty apartment less than moving, but the permanent exhibition that occupies the rest of the building effectively evokes the horror of the Nazi occupation and genocide.

Anne's diary has been translated into more than 50 languages and continues to be relevant in a 21st-century world where the dangers of anti-Semitism and racism are as prevalent as ever. Among those who have cited it as inspirational are South African leader Nelson Mandela, who read it while in prison under the apartheid regime. The book is perhaps most moving, and frightening, when it evokes an eerie sense of everyday life alongside the grotesque realities of Nazi-occupied Amsterdam.

Especially grim is the realization that Anne Frank, along with thousands of other concentration camp prisoners, came within weeks or months of surviving. She died, aged 14, in Bergen-Belsen camp in March 1945, less than six weeks before the arrival of Allied forces, the fall of Berlin, and the end of the World War II.

Anne Frank Huis
⊠ Prinsengracht 263
☎ 020 556 7100
✆ 020 620 7999
✈ reserveringen@annefrank.nl
🖳 www.annefrank.nl
🕑 09:00–17:00 daily (Sep–Mar); 09:00–21:00 daily (Apr–Aug)
💰 7.50 Euros
🚊 Tram 13, 17, 20; Bus 21, 170, 171, 172

Below: *The House at 263 Prinsengracht provided Anne Frank and her family with a secret refuge.*

Six Collection

✉ Amstel 218
☎ 020 674 7000, or
020 673 2121
📠 020 674 7001
✆ info@
rijksmuseum.nl
🖥 www.
rijksmuseum.nl
🕐 guided tours at
10:00 and 11:00 Mon,
Wed, Fri, but only by
appointment
💰 Admission free,
guided tours only
🚊 Tram 9, 14
Ⓜ Waterlooplein

See Map A–E5 | ★ ★ ★

SIX COLLECTION

Jan Six (1618–1700) was a patron of Rembrandt, and the artist's portrait of him, painted in 1654, is the centrepiece of this collection, housed in the home of the merchant dynasty which Six founded. One of the wealthiest merchant princes of 17th-century Amsterdam, Six became Burgomaster (Mayor) in 1690 at the age of 72.

Rembrandt's painting shows him in his prime, relaxed and self-confident. It is among the painter's finest works, with the added bonus that the Six Collection is rarely as crowded as the Rembrandt rooms of the Rijksmuseum, allowing visitors a little more time to contemplate the artist's work displayed in its gracious surroundings.

Below: *Jan Six, wealthy patron of Rembrandt.*

The building dates from 1680, and the collection also includes works by Frans Hals, Jacob van Ruisdael, Pieter Saenredam and a host of other masters. The Six family heirlooms on display also include some fine china and silverware and furniture, as a reminder of the style in which the wealthy families of 17th-century Amsterdam lived. Guided tours take place, but only by appointment. To book a tour, contact the Rijksmuseum (*see* page 14).

Six Collection & Willet Holthuysen

☀ See Map A–E5	★★★

WILLET HOLTHUYSEN MUSEUM

This beautifully preserved house at Herengracht 605 was built in 1687 for a member of the city council. Inside is a fine collection of ornaments, furniture and porcelain. Most of the exhibits are from the 19th century, when it was the home of Sandra Louise Gertruida Holthuysen and her husband Abraham Willet. The couple left the house and its contents to the city to be dedicated as a museum. They were inveterate collectors of antiques and *objets d'art*, all of which are there to be viewed, along with a fine collection of gleaming copper and china in the 18th-century basement kitchen.

Above: *The 17th-century façade of the Willet Holthuysen Museum.*

The rooms are lavishly decorated and the Louis XVI dining room, with its ornate furniture is particularly elegant. Abraham Willet's collection of delicate porcelain from Delft and the Hague is on display in a pretty room overlooking a trim garden lined with topiary. The upper floor bedrooms are now used to display other fine pieces of glass and silverware. Abraham's taste in paintings was less reliable. Most of those on display are mediocre.

Abraham and Louisa were fictionalized in the novel *Onpersoonlijke Hemmeringen* ('Impersonal Memories') by the Museum's first curator, Frans Coenen, in 1936, depicting Abraham in an unsympathetic light as a feckless spendthrift. He died in 1888, and when Louisa died seven years later she left the house, and his collection, to the city.

Willet Holthuysen Museum
⊠ Herengracht 605
☎ 020 523 1870
🖷 020 620 7784
⁀ info@willetholt
huysen.amsterdam.nl
🖳 www.willetholt
huysen.amsterdam.nl
🕘 10:00–17:00
Mon–Fri, 11:00–17:00
Sat–Sun
🔊 4 Euros
🚃 Tram 4, 9, 14
M Waterlooplein

⭐ *See* Map A–B2   ★★★

Above: *The gold-crowned Wester-toren towers over the Prinsengracht.*

WESTERKERK

The Westerkerk, with its tower crowned by a blue orb and crown and gilded weathervane, is considered the prettiest of Amsterdam's four 17th-century churches. It was begun by Hendrik de Keyser in 1619 and completed in 1638, after his death, by his son Pieter and Cornelis Dancker. The neoclassical interior designed by Jacob van Campen is in the shape of a double cross. The magnificent organ was decorated by Gerard de Lairesse, a pupil of Rembrandt's.

It is claimed that Rembrandt is buried in this church – his tomb is unmarked, but a plaque marks the grave of his son Titus.

The Westertoren (the church tower) is Amsterdam's tallest at 85m (251ft). From the top it offers a bird's-eye view of the city centre, its ring of canals, and the Jordaan district below. For reservations to visit the tower, contact the church office.

The church – which is the heart of Amsterdam's Presbyterian Dutch Reformed community – still plays an important part in the city's cultural life, with frequent organ recitals and a renowned performance each Good Friday of Bach's *St John Passion* by the resident Westerkerk Choir.

Westerkerk
✉ Prinsengracht 281
☎ 020 612 6856
(church office)
📠 020 427 6493
📧 info@westerkerk.nl
🖥 www@westerkerk.nl
🕐 10:00–16:00
Mon–Sat (Apr–Sep)
💰 Free
🚋 Tram 13, 14, 17

See Map B–G2   ★★

SCHEEPVAART MUSEUM

The Netherlands Maritime Museum has both indoor and outdoor exhibits, including replica 16th- and 17th-century sailing vessels. The main attraction is the square-rigger *Amsterdam*, a replica of an 18th-century Dutch East Indiaman.

In summer, the vessel is crewed by volunteer 'sailors', who attempt to recreate life at sea – swabbing the decks, cooking an authentically unappealing shipboard meal, firing off cannon and conducting a realistic sea burial, while on the quayside you can watch traditional sailmakers and boat-builders at work. The museum building dates from 1655 and was originally used by the Dutch admiralty as a warehouse.

Other high points of the museum include a re-creation of the vanished world of the great luxury passenger liners which – until air travel put them out of business – sailed regularly from Amsterdam to Asia and the Americas. There is also a lavishly decorated royal barge.

Scheepvaart Museum (Netherlands Maritime Museum)
⊠ Kattenburgerplein 1
☎ 020 523 2222
📠 020 523 2213
✒ info@scheepvaart museum.nl
🖳 www.scheepvaart museum.nl
🕓 10:00–17:00 Tue–Sun from mid-June to mid-Sep, also Mon from 10:00–17:00
💰 7.50 Euros
🚋 Tram 22, 28
🍽 Museum restaurant

Below: *The Maritime Museum overlooks the waters of the Oosterdok.*

Nieuwe Kerk
✉ Dam te Amsterdam
☎ 020 638 6909
📠 020 622 6649
📧 mail@nieuwekerk.nl
🖥 www.nieuwekerk.nl
🕐 11:00–18:00 daily
💰 Price varies according to exhibition
🚋 Tram: 51, 53, 54
Ⓜ Nieuwmarkt
🍴 't Nieuwe Kafe

See Map A–D2   ★★

NIEUWE KERK

New only in relation to the Oude Kerk (*see* page 21) this church dates from the late 15th century but has been restored after fires. The vaulted interior dates from the 17th century. Kings and queens of the Netherlands are crowned in the church, but it is now more an exhibition space than a place of worship, carrying a frequently changing programme of cultural displays. The carved Baroque pulpit and stained glass windows are worth a closer look.

One of the glories of the Nieuwe Kerk is its 10m (33ft) high pulpit, carved by the sculptor Albert Janszoon Vinckenbrinck over a period of 20 years between 1645 and 1664. The elaborate imagery includes six scenes representing biblical works of mercy, each presented as theatre scenes with three-dimensional wings, which give them remarkable visual depth. Vinckenbrink immortalized himself in his work as the model for the image of St Luke, the patron saint of painters and sculptors. The pulpit has its lighter side too – mischievous cherubs are sliding down the carved handrail.

Below: *The dignified Nieuwe Kerk, where kings and queens are crowned.*

⊙ *See* Map A–E2 ★★

MUSEUM AMSTELKRING

Chaplain's Bedroom
On your way to the attic church in the Amstelkring Museum look out for the chaplain's tiny bedroom, complete with cupboard-bed, patchwork quilt and chamber pot. On the bedside table are the chaplain's glasses, pipe and cap. The last Catholic chaplain to live here left in 1887 for more spacious quarters, but for two centuries this room was one of the 'perks' of the chaplain's job.

Left: *The Museum Amstelkring is one of the best preserved 17th-century townhouses in Amsterdam.*

The museum is housed in a 17th-century merchant's home. Each room is authentically furnished with the parlour in the style of the 18th century to the last detail. At the top of a narrow, ladder-like stair you step into a spacious and richly decorated place of worship. The attic of the house was the last of Amsterdam's *schuilkerks* or clandestine churches, and was known as Ons Lieve Heer op de Solder (Our Dear Lord in the Attic). In post-Reformation Amsterdam Catholic masses were outlawed, but once the first blaze of Protestant fervour faded they were tolerated in private. The church occupies the attics of three adjoining houses and with two galleries, an organ and religious paintings is far from the cramped refuge its name suggests.

Museum Amstelkring
✉ Oz Voorburgwal 40
☎ 020 624 6604
📠 020 638 1822
📧 info@museum
amstelkring.nl
🕐 10:00–17:00 Mon–
Sat, 13:00–17:00 Sun
💰 7.00 Euros
🚋 Tram 4, 9, 16,
24, 25
M Nieuwmarkt

⊙ *See* Map B–E4   ★★

ALBERT CUYPSTRAAT MARKET

Unlike the colourful, bohemian Waterlooplein market (*see* page 51), this is a practical and purposeful place, more dedicated to inner fortification than to outer adornment. As well as places to buy virtually anything you can eat (and the inhabitants of Amsterdam will eat virtually anything), there are also stalls selling the peculiar utensils for preparing everything from pickled herring to steamed rice.

This is the widest and busiest shopping street in the Old South, and its untidy, sprawling street market spills over into the surrounding streets for more than 1km (⅔ mile). It is a noisy, bustling expanse of stalls, shops and ethnic restaurants (mainly Indonesian and Surinamese) where, if you look hard enough, you can buy just about anything. It's a good place to stock up on Dutch coffee, cheeses, chocolates and other delicacies to take home.

Busy Cuypstraat is a happy hunting ground for pickpockets and bag snatchers. Keep a close eye on your purchases and valuables, especially when seated in cafés.

Albert Cuypstraat Market
⊠ Albert Cuypstraat/ Ferdinand Bolstraat
⊕ 09:30–17:00 Mon–Sat
🚋 Tram: 16, 20, 24, 25
🍽 there are numerous cafés and foods stalls on Albert Cuypstraat

See Map B–E4 | ★★

HEINEKEN BREWERY MUSEUM

Housed in the former Heineken Brewery, built in 1867, the museum is devoted to the beer which famously refreshes the 'parts other beers cannot reach'. Highlights include the stables, which still house heavy dray horses, the vast, gleaming copper brewing vats and, of course, the complimentary glass of beer at the end of your tour. Open for guided tours year-round. Only over 18s are allowed, and no reservations are possible.

The tour takes in the old brewing halls with their gleaming copper vats, stables with horses, coaches and brewers' drays, and other traditional and modern sections of the brewery that produces vast quantities of one of the world's favourite lager beers.

Heineken Experience
✉ Stadhouderskade 78
☎ 020 523 9666
📠 020 523 9441
✆ info@heineken experience.com
🖥 www.heineken experience.com
🕐 guided tours 09:00 and 11:00 Mon–Fri
💰 7.50 Euros
🚋 Tram 16, 24, 25
🍽 Bar-restaurant

Opposite: *Clothing and fresh produce on sale at Albert Cuypstraat market.*
Left: *Polished copper brew vats at the Heineken brewery.*

Above: *Zuiderkerk's tower affords great views of the city.*
Opposite: *The Tropenmuseum, a link with the east.*

St Nicolaas Day
St Nicolaas Kerk comes into its own on the feast of Saint Nicholas, held on the third Saturday of November with a picturesque festival gathering. Saint Nicholas, the patron saint of merchants and fishermen, naturally has a special place in the hearts of Amsterdammers. He is also the patron saint of children. In Dutch dialect he is called Sinterklaas, but he is more widely known around the world as Santa Claus.

Places of Worship
St Nicolaas Kerk

In an overwhelmingly Protestant city, St Nicolaas Kerk is one of the few prominent Catholic churches to be found. It was built between 1875 and 1887, much later than the other main churches of the city. However, despite its neo-Renaissance architecture it is a large, clumsy and looming building.
⊠ *Prins Hendrik-kade 76*
⏲ *09:30–17:30 daily Apr–Oct*
Ⓜ *Centraal Station*

Zuiderkerk

The Zuiderkerk's graceful spire and clock tower are embellished with red and gold dials. Designed in 1603 by Hendrik de Keyser, it was the city's first post-Reformation Protestant church and its spire is claimed to have inspired Sir Christopher Wren, architect of St Paul's Cathedral and other London churches. Inside is a disappointing permanent exhibition on town planning, but the tower is worth climbing for its views over the inner city.
⊠ *St Antoniesbree-straat*
☎ *020 622 2962*
⏲ *12:00–17:00 Mon–Fri, until 20:00 Thu; the tower is accessible 14:00–16:00 Wed–Sat, Jun–Sep*
Ⓜ *Waterlooplein*

Noorderkerk

The looming bulk of the Noorderkerk (North Church) is a prominent Amsterdam landmark. Built in

1620, it was designed by Hendrik de Keyser, architect of many of Amsterdam's Golden Age buildings, and Hendrik Jacobszoon Staets. A solid, well-proportioned building of brown brick and grey slate, it was De Keyser's last project. Its plan is that of a Greek cross, with four arms of equal length radiating from a centre crowned by one of De Keyser's trademark steeples.

✉ *Noordermarkt*
☎ *020 642 7819*
🕐 *10:00–16:00 Mon–Sat*
🚊 *Tram 1, 2, 5, 13, 17*

More places of worship on pages 20, 21, 28 and 30.

Museums
Allard Pierson Archaeological Museum

This museum's extensive collection from the ancient world includes mummies and bronzes from ancient Egypt, Roman statues, and Greek marbles and vases.

✉ *Oude Turfmarkt 127*
☎ *020 525 2556*
💻 *www.uba.uva.nl/apm*
🕐 *10:00–17:00 Tue–Fri, 13:00–17:00 weekends and holidays*

Tropenmuseum

Amsterdam's connection with the tropics goes back to the early years of the Dutch East India Company. Exhibits in the Museum of the Tropics recreate town and village streets from Asia, Africa, the Arab world, Polynesia and South America, with reconstructed buildings and recorded sounds and sights.

✉ *Linnaeusstraat 2*
☎ *020 568 8215*
🕐 *10:00–17:00 Mon–*
Fri, until 21:30 Tue, 12:00–17:00 Sat–Sun.
💰 *8 Euros*

Hash Marijuana Hemp Museum

This museum traces the positive aspects of marijuana and the cannabis plant through the ages and contrasts its medicinal, environmental and therapeutic benefits with the effects of legal drugs such as tobacco and alcohol.

✉ *Oudezijds Achterburgwal 130*
☎ *020 623 5961*
💻 *www.hash museum.com*
🕐 *11:00–20:00 Mon–Sat, 11:00–17:00 Sun*
🚊 *Tram: 4, 9, 16, 24, 25*

Taking Your Time
Making the most of the Museumplein needs two days – one for the Rijksmuseum (see page 14), a second for the Vincent van Gogh Museum (see page 16) and the Stedelijk (see page 18). All three these museums have cafeterias, and with a **Museumcard** you can step outside for a breath of fresh air, then go back to finish your tour. The treasures of Amsterdam's museums are much too fabulous to be rushed.

Opposite: *Van Loon Museum is set in beautiful gardens.*
Below: *The striking interior of the Trade Union Museum.*

Geels & Co. Koffie en Theemuseum

Geels, one of the city's longest-established importers, sells the best coffee in Amsterdam. A small museum traces the history of coffee and tea from the days of the Dutch East India Company.

✉ Warmoesstraat 67
☎ 020 624 0683
🕑 14:00–16:00 Tue and Fri, 14:00–16:30 Sat
💰 Free
🚋 Tram: 4, 19, 14, 16, 24, 25

Van Loon Museum

Built in 1672, the building was in the possession of the Van Loon family for several centuries, and is filled with family heirlooms, furniture and portraits of Van Loon ancestors from the 17th and 18th century. The house is not particularly striking, despite its historic associations (its first owner was Ferdinand Bol, a student of Rembrandt's, who lived here until 1680), but the family portraits illustrate the rise of an Amsterdam family from swashbuckling soldiers and privateers of the independence struggle to the dull, prosperous bourgeois in the 19th- and 20th-century paintings and photographs.

✉ Keisersgracht 672
☎ 020 624 5255
📠 020 427 4124
🖥 www.musvloon. box.nl
🕑 11:00–17:00 Mon– Tue, 13:00–17:00 Sun
💰 5 Euros
🚋 Tram 16, 24, 25

Nationaal Vakbondsmuseum

Known as 'De Burcht van Berlage' (Berlage's Castle), the Trade Union Museum is one of Amsterdam's most elegant buildings. Commissioned by the General Netherlands Diamond Workers Union and completed in 1900, it was designed by H.P. Berlage. The collection and displays centre on the history of the Dutch trade union movement and the diamond cutting industry. The

striking interior, with its splendid staircase, decorative brickwork and soaring arches, grand council room and boardroom with fine murals by the Dutch Impressionist painter Roland Holst, is finely preserved.

⊠ *Henri Polaklaan 9*
☎ *020 624 1166*
✆ *020 623 7331*
▱ *www.deburcht.nl*
🕐 *11:00–17:00 Tue–Fri,*
13:00–17:00 Sat–Sun
💰 *5 Euros*
🚋 *Tram 9, 14*

Hollandsche Schouwburg

This museum was built in 1897 as a venue for light opera, then became the main venue for the early 20th-century revival of Dutch theatre. During World War II, the Nazis used it as a concentration camp assembly point for Dutch Jews, who were sent from here to the transit camp at Westerbork, then to the death camps of Sobibor and Auschwitz. Since the 1960s the empty,

pilastered façade of the theatre has been kept as a ghostly memorial to the victims of the Holocaust. The restored part of the museum includes an exhibition room with videos and documents from the era of Nazi occupation and the deportations. There is a small memorial garden behind the museum.

⊠ *Plantage Midden-laan 24*
☎ *020 531 0340*
✆ *020 531 0311*
▱ *www.hollandsche schouwburg.nl*
🕐 *11:00–16:00 daily*
💰 *Free*
🚋 *Tram 4, 9, 14, 16*

Museumwerf 't Kromhout

This dockyard, now the open-air Kromhout Wharf Museum, first served the Dutch merchant fleet in the 18th century. By the early 20th century it was building and fitting diesel engines for most of the country's vast fleet of canal barges. Recently renovated.

⊠ *Hoogte Kadijk 147*
☎/✆ *020 627 6777*
▱ *www.machine kamer.nl*
🕐 *10:00–15:00 Tue*

💰 *3.70 Euros*
Ⓜ *Centraal Station*

Nederlands Filmmuseum

On the outside it's a pretty 19th-century pavilion, very much in tune with its surroundings on the fringe of the Vondelpark. Inside, it is a picture palace from the first golden age of moving pictures. The interior of the Cinema Parisien, Amsterdam's first movie theatre, was salvaged from demolition in 1987 and has been painstakingly restored within the museum. There are three screenings of new and classic films every day and an ever-changing programme of interesting exhibitions on the development of cinema.

✉ *Vondelpark 3*
☎/📠 *020 589 1400*
🖳 *www.film museum.nl*
🕓 *12:00–19:00 daily (exhibitions), 19:30–21:30 daily (film)*
💰 *Films 7.80 Euros, exhibitions 2 Euros*

Woonbootmuseum

Located on board the *Hendrika Maria*, the Houseboat Museum gives you a look into life on the water.
✉ *Opposite Prinsengracht 296*
☎ *020 427 0750*
🕓 *10:00–17:00 Tue–Sun*
💰 *3 Euros*
🚋 *Tram 4, 9, 14, 16, 20*

Theatermuseum

This museum has an eclectic collection of memorabilia ranging from costumes, posters and an 18th-century miniature theatre to machines used to produce alarming sound and lighting effects. The ground floor rooms are decorated with early 18th-century murals depicting biblical scenes.
✉ *Herengracht 168*
☎ *020 551 3300*
📠 *020 551 3303*
🖳 *www.tin.nl*
🕓 *11:00–17:00 Tue–Fri, 13:00– 17:00 Sat–Sun*
💰 *3.70 Euros*
🚋 *Tram 13, 14, 17*

Bijbels Museum

The Bible Museum is a collection devoted to retelling the stories of the Old and New Testaments. The models of the Holy Land, Jerusalem and the Temple of Solomon are none too exciting but the elegance of the simple, 18th-century wooden interior is worth a visit.
✉ *Herengracht 366*
☎ *020 624 2436*
📠 *020 624 8355*
🖳 *www.bijbels museum.nl*
🕓 *10:00–17:00 Mon–Sat, 13:00–17:00 Sun*
💰 *6 Euros*
🚋 *Tram 1, 2, 5*

Versetzmuseum

This museum, devoted to World War II Dutch resistance, is housed in a former synagogue. It has an interesting exhibition of photographs, video and audio tapes.
✉ *Plantage Kerklaan 61*
☎/📠 *020 620 2535*
🖳 *www.versetz museum.org*

🕐 *10:00–17:00 Tue–Fri,*
11:00–17:00 weekends

🧴 *3.70 Euros*

🚊 *Tram 6, 9, 14, 20A*

More museums on pages 14, 16, 18, 19, 22, 23, 25, 26, 27, 29, 31 and 33.

Green Spaces
The Vondelpark

This park, a long 48ha (120-acre) rectangle of lawns, trees and lakes slanting south-west from the Singel-gracht, was land-scaped in the late 19th century. The generous sweeps of pathway and wood-land are interspersed with eccentrically shaped stretches of water lined with weeping willows and crossed by toy-like bridges – each a scene from a willow-pattern teacup. It is a lively place, especially in summer, when it becomes a magnet for sunbathers, kite-fliers, frisbee-players, musicians and street entertainers. In the late 1960s and early 70s it became a mecca for the European counter-culture, with thousands of people camping and creating a summer-long festi-val atmosphere, but the hippy dream went sour, with a growth in robberies and hard drug use leading to

> **Joost van Vondel**
> Joost van Vondel (1582–1674) was to Dutch poetry and drama what his near contemporary Rem-brandt was to painting; indeed, one of the scenes from his tower-ing drama *Gijsbrecht van Amstel* is claimed to have provided the painter with the inspiration for *The Night Watch*. Like Rembrandt, Van Vondel too went from rags to riches and back again, ending his days on a state pension.

Below: *The Vondel-park is a lovely green oasis in the heart of the city.*

Tulips
The Dutch obsession with tulips dates from the mid-16th century, when the first bulbs and flowers were brought back from their native Turkey ('tulip' means 'turban' in Turkish). They quickly became a national obsession, and when a Leiden horticulturalist named **Johan van Hoogheland** discovered how to hybridize them to produce different shapes and colours, tulip mania reached new heights. Multicoloured varieties appeared on the scene; red, pink and white blooms were most highly prized. Bulb-growers set out to produce ever more flamboyant varieties and prices soared. By the mid-1630s speculation in tulip futures was rife, leading eventually to a market crash which left many growers bankrupt before a more realistic attitude asserted itself. Tulips are on sale everywhere in Amsterdam and in particular at the **Bloemenmarkt** (see page 52). The best place to see tulips outside of Amsterdam is at the Keukenhof.

police cracking down on sleeping in the park. Popular open-air rock concerts and the impromptu jewellery sellers who flock here on a summer Sunday give the park an agreeably off-beat feel. Overlooking the largest lake is the bizarre Ronde Blauwe Theehuis (Round Blue Teahouse), a fine specimen of 1930s functionalist architecture. A statue commemorating poet and playwright Joost van Vondel stands at the entrance. Landmarks in the park include the Openlucht Theater (Open-Air Theatre) where from Jun to Aug there are open-air performances by all sorts of musicians.

Martin Luther Kingpark
This park overlooks the Amstel where it curves southwest by Utrechtsebrug.

Right: *Poet and playwright Joost van Vondel is commemorated by a statue at the entrance to the Vondelpark.*

Sport and Recreation

Left: Many locals use the canals, and their bicycles, for recreation as well as for transport.

ACTIVITIES
Sport and Recreation

Amsterdammers and the Dutch in general are not fanatical about sport, though **soccer** is popular, with both the city's own team **Ajax Amsterdam** and the national team ranking highly in European and international championships.

During an exceptionally hard winter the canals may freeze hard enough for Amsterdammers to get their **skates** on, but most years only the rural canals of the northern Netherlands, a couple of hours drive away, are solid enough for skating.

Amsterdam boasts 550,000 **bicycles** – more than one per household. Ranks of bikes stand padlocked outside Centraal Station every day, and on Amsterdam's flat streets they are a quiet, effortless and non-polluting way of getting around. You can rent bicycles by the day from a number of outlets in the city centre, and a bike is the ideal way to travel independently around the city centre.

Next to the Martin Luther Kingpark (*see page 40*) is De Mirandabad, a large complex of indoor and outdoor **swimming pools**.

Best Beaches

Few visitors think of the Netherlands as a seaside country, but the Dutch know that for two brief months of summer sunshine their North Sea coasts offer long stretches of clean sand, sunbathing, swimming and plenty of seaside entertainment. Amsterdam's nearest beach is at **Zandvoort**, about 40 minutes away by train (15 minutes from Haarlem). The central stretch of beach is naturally the busiest, but the further you walk from town the less crowded it gets. The Hague, too, has a splendid beach at **Scheveningen**.

Alternative Amsterdam
The Old Side and Red Light District

This part of the city presents some of Amsterdam's oddest contrasts. At its upper end are the fleshpots of the city's red light district, known as **De Walletjes**, where the glass windows of the shops display near-naked or provocatively clad women and transvestites who rap on the windows to beckon passers-by. In stark contrast, overlooking them are some of Amsterdam's most prominent churches.

During daylight the sex shops, massage parlours and go-go bars just look sad and seedy; meanwhile, everyday life goes on around them, the ordinary inhabitants of the Old Side apparently oblivious to the ubiquitous sleaze. At night, the glow of coloured neon lends the whole scene a spurious glamour and excitement.

The **Casa Rosso Erotic Theatre** claims to be 'one of the most superior erotic shows in the world with a tremendous choreography and a touch of class'. It is at least marginally less sleazy than some of the dis-

---

Cough-ins

During the 1960s the Spui was the meeting place of the Provos, an anarchic hippy movement. They held 'cough-ins' around the Lieverdje statue – given to the city by a major cigarette company – to highlight the dangers of smoking, crammed cigarette vending machines with fake marijuana cigarettes, and – more sensibly – campaigned for free housing for young families, free contraception and abortion clinics, and free 'white bicycles' for use by all. The white bicycle plan was actually introduced, but most of the bikes vanished almost overnight, no doubt to be repainted by their new owners.

trict's smaller and more obvious rip-off joints. Near the Casa Rosso is the **Erotic Museum**. It advertises five floors of 'erotic enjoyment and arts' celebrating all that makes De Walletjes notorious, from postcards, books and videos to an entire floor devoted to sado-masochism.

The Eel Riots

The Lindengracht canal was the scene of a riot when on 25 July 1886 an officious policeman tried to halt a traditional eel-pulling contest (a sort of tug of war using a live eel smeared with soap to make it even more slippery). The crowd objected, the policeman was bundled into a cellar and police reinforcements were showered with flowerpots and roof-tiles. Eventually the army was called in to restore order. In the three-day riot, 26 people were killed and hundreds more injured.

> **Casa Rosso Erotic Theatre**
> ✉ Oudezijds Voorburgwal 106–108
> ☎ 020 627 8954
> ⏰ 20:00–02:00 daily; weekends until 03:00
>
> **Erotic Museum**
> ✉ Oudezijds Achterburgwal 54
> ☎ 020 624 7303
> ⏰ 11:00–13:00 Mon–Thu and Sun, 11:00–14:00 Fri–Sat

> **Pornography**
> Amsterdam has no inhibitions about what kind of pictorial material may be openly displayed, and some of the video packaging, books and postcards in shop windows are extremely anatomically explicit. If this kind of thing repels you, steer clear of the Nieuwendijk, which has more than its fair share of sleaze, and the Walletjes area, the heart of the red light district.

Opposite: *Cannabis Connoisseurs Club is a landmark of Amsterdam's laid-back marijuana-smoking subculture.*
Left: *The Casa Rosso Theatre is the city's best-known strip-tease club.*

**Amsterdam's High-
lights Walking Tour**
Location: Maps A and B
Distance: about 3km
(2 miles)
Duration: one day
Start: Brouwersgracht
Finish: Museumplein

A Life Apart
Born in 1853, **Vincent
van Gogh** painted for
less than 10 years of
his short life. Looking
at the glowing works
on display in the
Rijksmuseum Vincent
van Gogh, it is hard to
believe that his genius
was barely recognized
during his lifetime. He
sold only one painting
in his lifetime, and lived
almost entirely on
advances from his
younger brother **Theo**,
an art dealer, who
managed to make a far
better living selling
paintings than Vincent
did painting them. Theo
also died young, at the
age of 32, and it was
Theo's widow **Johanna**
who finally brought
Vincent's work to a
wider audience. Not
long after his death,
his paintings began to
fetch high prices from
galleries and collectors
worldwide.

Walking Tours
Amsterdam's Highlights
To take in Amsterdam's highlights in a full
day's walking, walk from **Brouwersgracht**
down Prinsengracht to the **Noorderkerk**
(see page 34). Crossing the Prinsenstraat
bridge, walk down the east bank to **Anne
Frank Huis** (see page 25) and the **Westerkerk** (see page 28). A detour along Raadhuisstraat takes you to the **Royal Palace**
(see page 17). From here take Nieuwezijds
Voorburgwal to the **Amsterdam Historical
Museum** (see page 19), the **Begijnhof** (see
page 20) and the **Spui** (see pages 51–52),
crossing the Singel to visit the **Bloemenmarkt** (see page 52). Walk south on Leidsestraat, cross the Herengracht and walk
along the south bank to Nieuwe Spiegel-
straat, then down the Spiegelgracht and
across the Lijnbaangracht and Singelgracht
canals to reach **Museumplein**, site of the
Van Gogh Museum (see page 16) and the
Rijksmuseum (see page 14).

Right: *The Begijnhof
is the site of the
oldest house in
Amsterdam.*

The Jewish Quarter

To the east of old Amsterdam and the Walletjes is the former Jewish quarter, where Rembrandt lived and painted and where Sephardic and Ashkenazi communities flourished from the 17th century until the Holocaust.

From Nieuwmarket and its 15th-century weigh-gate, the **Waag**, take a walk down St Antoniebreestraat to the **Zuiderkerk** (*see* page 34). Then turn left up Oude Schans for a look at the venerable **Montelbaanstoren** – a favourite subject of Rembrandt's. Turn sharp right at the end, and cross the **Peperbrug** or Pepper Bridge – it gets its name from the spices that used to be stored in the nearby warehouses in the heyday of the Dutch East India Company. Walk down Nieuw Ullenburgstraat, pausing for a visit to the **Gassan diamond factory**, then go down Jodenbreestraat to **Rembrandt's house** at No 4–6 (*see* page 22). From here, stroll through the daily **Waterlooplein Market**, before finishing your walk with a visit to the **Joods Historisch Museum** and the **Portuguese Synagogue**, off Mr Visserplein (*see* page 23).

Above: *The Montelbaanstoren was the subject of many of Rembrandt's drawings and etchings.*

<u>**The Jewish Quarter Walking Tour**</u>
Location: Map A
Distance: about 5km (2.5 miles)
Duration: 3–4 hours
Start: Nieuwmarkt Metro
Finish: Waterlooplein Metro

Right: *Dutch fields are a sea of colour in spring.*
Opposite: *Ethnological exhibit at the Tropenmuseum.*

Organized Tours

A wide range of guided tours and excursions within Amsterdam and to neighbouring parts of the Netherlands is offered by an equally wide range of tour companies. Cycling tours and canal cruising are also offered. Half-day excursions can include trips to the **Zaanse Schans**, a pretty windmill village, and to **Volendam** and **Marken**, fishing villages on the shores of the Ijsselmeer, **Delft**, **The Hague** and **Scheveningen**, as well as the famous **Keukenhof flower gardens** (Apr–May). These gardens, situated near Lisse, are one of the most popular excursions from Amsterdam and can be reached by train or bus. The gardens are open only in spring, when you can see six million tulips, narcissi, daffodils and hyacinths in full colourful glory.

Several options are available for tours around Amsterdam's canals. The **Canal Bus** boat service operates circular canal routes from Centraal Station with stops at Anne Frank Huis, Keizersgracht/Raadhuisstraat, Leidseplein, and the Rijksmuseum. Canal pedal boats can be rented from **Canal Bike** or **Roell Canal Boats**.

Fun for Children

Families with children should plan to visit the Netherlands in summer, when there are plenty of open-air attractions in and around Amsterdam. Many of these are in the eastern part of the city. Try **Artis Zoo and Museum** (*see* page 48), with thousands of birds and animals; the **Hortus Botanicus Amsterdam** (*see* page 24), with its huge

Canal Transport
Canal Bus
☎ 020 623 9886

Canal Bike
✉ Weteringschans 24
☎ 020 626 5574

Roell Canal Boats
✉ Mauritskade
☎ 020 692 9124

Information and Passes
Public transport information, maps and tickets are available from
VVV Amsterdam Tourist Office
☎ 020 551 2525
✆ info@amsterdam tourist.nl
🖥 www.amsterdam tourist.nl
🖥 www.visit amsterdam.nl
and from **GVB** offices,
✉ Stationsplein
🕐 07:00–19:00 Mon–Fri, 08:00–19:00 weekends; and at
✉ Prins Hendrikkade 108–114, 🕐 08:30–16:30 Mon–Fri.
Public transport information,
☎ 0900 92 92.
The **All Amsterdam Transport Pass** offers unlimited travel by tram, bus, boat and metro and is available at the GVB ticket office at Prins Hendrikkade 108–114 and at Canal Bus moorings at Rijksmuseum, Leidseplein, Centraal Station and Anne Frank House.

Kindermuseum
✉ Linnaeusstraat 2
☎ 020 568 8300
🕑 tours Sun and public
holidays at 12:15,
13:30 and 14:45

Artis Zoo and Museum
✉ Plantage Kerklaan 38–40
☎ 020 523 3400
🖥 www.artis.nl
🕑 09:00–17:00
Mon–Sat, museum closed Mon

New Metropolis Science and Technology Centre
✉ Oosterdok 2
☎ 0900 919 1100
🕑 10:00–18:00
Sun–Thu, 10:00–21:00
Fri–Sat

Madame Tussaud's Wax Museum
✉ Dam 20
☎ 020 523 0623
🕑 10:00–17:30 daily
Sep–Jun, 09:30–19:30
daily Jul–Aug

hothouses full of strange tropical plants; **Tropenmuseum** (see page 35), with its fascinating dioramas; and the **Kindermuseum** (see below), dedicated to younger visitors. Children will also enjoy the spectacle of the **guards** at the Koninklijk Paleis (see page 17).

Kindermuseum

Housed within the Tropenmuseum, the Kindermuseum (Children's Museum) is specially targeted at 6- to 12-year-olds and has a programme of guided tours and displays on similar themes to the Tropenmuseum. Reservation is essential for the tours.

Artis Zoo and Museum

Founded in 1838, Artis is the oldest zoo on the European continent, with 900 animal species and a wealth of plant life. The zoo's paths are dotted with statues, most of them commemorating obscure Dutch botanists and zoologists. Larger animals are in the eastern half of the zoo. A planetarium, geological and zoological museums, an aquarium and a children's playground

complement the animals. The Zoological Museum, which is housed in the aquarium building, has no permanent display but operates a programme of changing exhibitions.

New Metropolis Science and Technology Centre (NEMO)

Looking like a grounded spaceship in the middle of the Oosterdok, this new attraction is packed with hands-on experiments in science, engineering and electronics and is ideal for kids of all ages.

Madame Tussaud's Wax Museum

At the Amsterdam version of Madame Tussaud's wax museum, special effects recreate the sounds and sights (though fortunately not the smells) of the city three centuries ago. For contrast, there are also 20th-century displays and an array of effigies of pop stars, politicians and celebrities.

Madame Tussaud Scenerama

Lifelike replicas of celebrities, sporting heroes and historical figures are on display at this venue.

Electric Ladyland

Situated to the west of Prinsengracht, the world's first museum of fluorescent art in dazzling colours also has amazing displays of fluorescent minerals.

Above: *The gateway to Artis, Europe's oldest zoo.*
Opposite: *The last of Amsterdam's street organs will captivate younger children.*

Madame Tussaud's Scenerama
✉ Dam 7
☎ 020 622 9239
🕐 10:00–17:30 daily Sep–Jun, 09:30–19:30 daily Jul–Aug

Electric Ladyland
✉ corner of Egelantiersgracht and Tweede Leliedwarsstraat
☎ 020 420 3776
🕐 13:00–18:00 Tue–Sat

Above: *Magna Plaza, a shopper's temple.*
Opposite: *The market at Waterlooplein.*

Diamonds

Amsterdam became a centre of the diamond trade in the late 16th century, when its rival Antwerp – then Europe's diamond capital – was sacked by the Spanish. Many of the Antwerp traders fled to Amsterdam, taking their skills and trading contacts with them. Amsterdam remained the diamond capital till World War II, when most of the the the city's Jewish workers were deported and murdered by the German occupiers. Ironically, postwar Antwerp won back leadership of the world diamond market it lost 350 years earlier.

Shopping

Like all the major European tourist cities, central Amsterdam is dominated by shops selling the tackiest of souvenirs. Some visitors may be surprised to find explicit pornography openly on sale next to postcards, camera film and T-shirts. However, Amsterdam also has some excellent shopping opportunities for art, antiques and curios, which are on sale in established galleries and auction rooms, and also at the various regular markets around the city.

Diamonds

Amsterdam is a world diamond centre, and many of the city's diamond polishers offer free cutting demonstrations as well as sales of set and unset stones. Main outlets are:

Amsterdam Diamond Centre, ⊠ 1 Rokin, ☎ 020 624 5787.

Bonebakker, ⊠ 88–90 Rokin, ☎ 020 623 2294.

Coster Diamonds, ⊠ 2–6 Paulus Potterstraat, ☎ 020 676 2222.

Gassan Diamonds, ⊠ 173–175 Nieuwe Uilenburgerstraat, ☎ 020 622 5333.

Van Moppes and Zoon, ✉ 2–6 Albert Cuypstraat, ☎ 020 676 1242.
Principal Diamonds, ✉ 3 Tweede Weteringdwarstraat, ☎ 020 624 3417.
Rokin Diamonds, ✉ 12 Rokin, ☎ 020 624 7973.
Stoeltie Diamonds, ✉ 13–17 Wagenstraat, ☎ 020 623 7601.

Clothes

Stylish designer stores are to be found in the Oud Zuid (Old South) part of town. Beethovenstraat, Van Baerlestraat and PC Hoofstraat are the places to look for international designer names, fashionable boutiques, jewellers, exclusive shoe shops and accessories.

Arts and Antiques

Antique dealers and galleries cluster near the Rijksmuseum along the Spiegelgracht, a short canal lined by almost 100 antique shops. A full list is available from VVV Amsterdam Tourist Board.

Shops
Magna Plaza

This palatial building, with its elaborate bell tower, turrets, onion-domes and leering gargoyles, is a classic of imitation Dutch Renaissance style. Built in 1908 as the main post office, it looks more like a fairy-tale palace than anything else. The stone colonnades and galleries of its interior are richly adorned with shields, crests and gargoyles. It has been converted into an up-market shopping mall.
✉ *Nieuwezijds Voorburgwal 182*

Markets
Waterlooplein

The daily market held here, though colourful enough, is a mere shadow of the original **flea market** which developed at the very heart of the Jewish quarter. It has an intriguing clutter of stalls selling neo-hippy gear, cheap jewellery, junk, old clothes and perhaps even the occasional genuine antique. ⏰ *09:00–17:00 Mon–Fri, 08:30–17:30 Sat.*

Spui Kunstmarkt

The Spui Art Market has booths selling everything from pretty ceramics to surrealist oils. The quality of the work varies wildly:

some is exciting and adventurous, some competent but uninspired, and some without discernible merit.
⊠ *The Spui*
🕑 *10:00–18:00 Sun Apr–Nov*

Spui Boekenmarkt

The Spui Book Market is crammed with stalls selling antiquarian books and prints.
⊠ *The Spui*
🕑 *10:00–18:00 Fri*

Nieuwmarkt

Nieuwmarkt is a wide and somewhat bleak brick-cobbled square enlivened by a row of cafés and coffee shops, a scattering of snack stalls and the weekly **antique market**.
🕑 *09:00–17:00 Sun, May–Sep*

Bloemenmarkt

This small floating market comprises a single row of pontoon-booths and is one of Amsterdam's most photographed tourist attractions. Various enclosed booths open onto the street, so their floral glories are hidden till you reach the Bloemenmarkt quay.
⊠ *Singelgracht, opposite Muntplein*
🕑 *09:30–17:00 Mon–Sat*

Thorbeckeplein Art Market

Like the Spui Art Market, the standard of the works displayed here is a matter of pot luck, but there is always something different to look at.
⊠ *Thorbeckeplein*
🕑 *10:30–18:00 Sun Mar–Oct*

Boerenmarkt

This is the place to find cheeses, herbs, honey, freshly baked seed-flavoured bread, or a dozen kinds of wild fungus.
⊠ *square between the Noorderkerk and the Prinsengracht*
🕑 *09:00–17:00 Sat (until 15:00 in winter)*

Noordermarkt

This market sells old and new clothes, jewellery and bric-a-brac. If you are looking for an antique leather jacket, a beat-

up fedora, or something in velvet and old lace, this is the place to start.

⊠ *north side of the Noorderkerk*

🕘 *09:00–17:00 Mon*

Antiquemarkt de Looier

The Looier Antique Market is a labyrinth of stalls piled high with the clutter of centuries. Some stalls are permanent fixtures, specializing in a favourite genre – antique brassware, say, or glass bottles, or jewellery. Others seem to stock anything that is old.

⊠ *Elandsgracht 109*

🕘 *11:00–17:00 Sat– Wed, 11:00–21:00 Thu*

Rommelmarkt

Close to De Looier market is an even more glorious permanent jumble sale, the Looiersgracht Flea Market. It seems that this is where items end up when they have failed to find a buyer in one of the many other city

markets. This market is at its best on Saturday and Sunday, when you never know what you will find. Most weekend visitors to the Rommelmarkt are Amsterdammers in search of bargain clothes, furniture or bric-a-brac, often accompanied by a few eagle-eyed antique dealers hunting the stalls for special finds to be sold at a handsome profit. Wednesday is also a jumble day; Monday it becomes a coin and stamp market, Tuesday is set aside for books and records and Thursday for used and antique clothes.

⊠ *Looiersgracht 38*

🕘 *11:00–17:00 Sat–Thu*

Above: *Browsing among the clothing can yield bargains.*
Opposite: *All the colours of the rainbow are found at the Bloemenmarkt.*

Postzegelmarkt
This is an entertaining Stamp Market for stampo collectors.
⊠ along Nieuwezijds Voorburgwal
🕘 13:00–16:00 Wed and Sat

Duty-free
Amsterdam Schiphol Airport has a very extensive duty-free shopping area. For a shopping catalogue write or fax
Dept SGE,
⊠ PO Box 7501, 1118 ZG, Amsterdam Schiphol Airport
📞 020 601 2967

Above: *The Amstel Hotel, one of the city's finest, a grand edifice on the banks of the River Amstel.*

Houseboats

Houseboats are one of the instantly recognized symbols of Amsterdam. About 2400 officially registered houseboats are moored along Amsterdam's canals. In the postwar years, when the city suffered a severe housing shortage, floating homes were a cheap alternative to rented apartments. These days they are eagerly sought after and are no longer cheap. Many are built on the wooden hulls of old Dutch barges, but most are erected on a concrete pontoon. Almost all have piped gas, electricity and all the other modern conveniences.

WHERE TO STAY

Amsterdam has a very wide choice of places to stay, from five-star international chain hotels to cheap dormitories for budget travellers. However accommodation is comparatively expensive at all levels, with demand matching or exceeding supply almost all year round. The **VVV Tourist Office** at Amsterdam Centraal Station can find accommodation at all price levels.

In a **luxury** (four- or five-star) hotel you can expect services and facilities up to the highest international standards. Many of the best city-centre hotels, however, are in historic buildings, and rooms in these can be smaller than in the newer luxury hotels.

Three-star hotels offer high standards of service, decor and in-room facilities. Most have a breakfast room but few include restaurants and you are unlikely to find facilities such as swimming pools, health centres or business centres.

Two- and **one-star** hotels offer simple accommodation, with some en suite rooms having a shower and WC but no bath, and others with shared bathrooms and WCs.

City Centre

• *LUXURY*

Amsterdam Renaissance Hotel
(Map A–D1)
In the old city centre, close to Centraal Station and many of the museums; overlooks the canal.
✉ *Kattengat 1*
☎ *020 621 2223*
📠 *020 627 5245*

Blakes Hotel Amsterdam
(Map A–B4)
The city's newest and most luxurious (and therefore expensive) boutique hotel.
✉ *Keizersgracht 384*
☎ *020 530 2010*
📠 *020 530 2030*

Seven One Seven
(Map A–B5)
New five-star bed and breakfast; enjoy it in total comfort.
✉ *Prinsengracht 717*
☎ *020 427 0717*
📠 *020 427 0718*

Golden Tulip Barbizon Palace
(Map A–F2)
Luxury hotel behind the façades of a row of 17th-century houses, opposite Centraal Station.
✉ *Prins Hendrikkade 59–72*
☎ *020 556 4564*
📠 *020 624 3353*

Hotel de L'Europe
(Map A–D4)
This is Amsterdam's most luxurious hotel, built in 1896 and renovated in 1993; a model of 19th-century elegance and modern comfort. It overlooks the Amstel, the Munttoren and the Bloemenmarkt.
✉ *Nieuwe Doelenstraat 2–8*
☎ *020 531 1777*
📠 *020 531 1778*

The Grand
(Map A–D3)
Built in 1578 as a royal inn, then used as Amsterdam's city hall, The Grand is a monument in its own right. Very modern within, with facilities including a superb pool and health centre and a stylish canal-front haute cuisine restaurant, Café Roux.

✉ *Oudezijds Voorburgwal 197*
☎ *020 555 3111*
📠 *020 555 3222*

Crowne Plaza Amsterdam City Centre (Map A–E1)
Luxury chain hotel located in the heart of the old city.
✉ *Nieuwezijds Voorburgwal 5*
☎ *020 620 0500*
📠 *020 620 1173*

Golden Tulip Grand Hotel Krasnapolsky
(Map A–D3)
Built in 1866, this five-star hotel opposite the Royal Palace is a favourite Amsterdam rendezvous.
✉ *Dam 9*
☎ *020 554 9111*
📠 *020 622 8607*

Hotel Pulitzer
(Map A–B4)
The Hotel Pulitzer has been created from 24 elegant canalside houses and each of its 231 rooms is decorated with original works of art. It overlooks the Prinsengracht.

✉ *Prinsengracht 315-331*
☎ *020 523 5235*
📠 *020 627 6753*

Radisson SAS Hotel Amsterdam

(Map A–E4)
This modern hotel, with its canal views, was built in 1990 within several 19th-century buildings.
✉ *Rusland 17*
☎ *020 623 1231*
📠 *020 520 8200*

American Hotel

(Map A–B6)
The American is one of Amsterdam's most famous luxury hotels, overlooking the Leidseplein.
✉ *Leidsekade 97*
☎ *020 556 3000*
📠 *020 556 3001*

Swissôtel Amsterdam Ascot

(Map A–D3)
Built behind a 19th-century façade, this is a comfortable business hotel located in the heart of the city.
✉ *Damrak 96*
☎ *020 522 3000*
📠 *020 522 3223*

Canal Crown Hotel

(Map A–D5)
New small hotel in a historic building on the Herengracht.
✉ *Herengracht 519–525*
☎ *020 420 0055*
📠 *020 420 0993*

Hotel Estheréa

(Map A–C4)
This comfortable, family-owned four-star hotel is housed in 17th-century buildings.
✉ *Singel 303–309*
☎ *020 624 5146*
📠 *020 623 9001*

Jolly Hotel Carlton

(Map A–D5)
Next to the Amstel, Munttoren and the Bloemenmarkt, four-star hotel belonging to an Italian chain.
✉ *Vijzelstraat 4*
☎ *020 622 2266*
📠 *020 626 6183*

Die Port van Cleve

(Map A–D2)
Comfortable four-star hotel which houses 'De Poort', Amsterdam's most famous historic restaurant.

✉ *Nieuwezijds Voorburgwal 176–180*
☎ *020 624 4860*
📠 *020 622 0240*

Victoria Hotel Amsterdam

(Map A–E2)
A central four-star hotel conveniently located opposite Centraal Station.
✉ *Damrak 1–5*
☎ *020 623 4255*
📠 *020 625 2997*

• *MID-RANGE*

Ambassade Hotel

(Map A–C4)
Comfortable hotel with lots of character and a central location on the Herengracht. Excellent value.
✉ *Herengracht 335–353*
☎ *020 626 2333*
📠 *020 624 5321*

Canal House Hotel

(Map A–C2)
Elegant three-star hotel in a 17th-century building. The rooms are furnished with antiques.
✉ *Keizersgracht 148*
☎ *020 622 5182*
📠 *020 624 1317*

Cok City Hotel

(Map A–D2)

Conveniently located three-star hotel.

✉ Nieuwezijds Voorburgwal 50
☎ 020 422 0011
📠 020 420 0357

Eden Hotel Amsterdam

(Map A–E5)

This comfortable, well located three-star is situated between the Amstel and Rembrandtplein.

✉ Amstel 144
☎ 020 530 7878
📠 020 624 2946

Mercure Arthur Frommer (Map B–E3)

Part of the three-star French chain, this hotel is close to the Noorderkerk and named after the doyen of budget travel guidebook writers.

✉ Noorderstraat 46
☎ 020 622 0328
📠 020 622 3208

• BUDGET

Rokin (Map A–D4)

Two-star hotel, located near the Dam and the Royal Palace.

✉ Rokin 73
☎ 020 626 7485
📠 020 625 6453

City Hotel Amsterdam

(Map A–F3)

This two-star hotel is close to Centraal Station.

✉ Prins Hendrikkade 130
☎ 020 623 0836
📠 020 638 3799

Multatuli

(Map A–D1)

Good-value two-star near the station, clean and bright.

✉ Prins Hendrikkade 12, ☎ 020 627 4282
📠 020 620 8003

Imperial (Map A–E5)

A pleasantly located two-star situated near the museums.

✉ Thorbeckeplein 9
☎ 020 622 0051
📠 020 624 5836

De Korenaer

(Map A–D2)

Very central two-star opposite the station.

✉ Damrak 50
☎ 020 622 0855
📠 020 620 7685

A-Train Hotel

(Map A–E1)

This labyrinthine one-star hotel has tiny rooms but is very handy for the station and coffee shops.

✉ Prins Hendrikkade 23, ☎ 020 624 1942
📠 020 622 7759.

Outside the Centre

• LUXURY

Amstel Inter-Continental Amsterdam

(Map B–F3)

This historic hotel opened in 1667 and was renovated in 1992. The elegant building overlooks the River Amstel.

✉ Prof. Tulpplein 1
☎ 020 622 6060
📠 020 622 5808

Le Meridien Apollo

(Map B–C5)

This business hotel is close to Museumplein and very convenient for the RAI conference centre and the World Trade Centre.

✉ Apollolaan 2
☎ 020 673 5922
📠 020 570 5744

Classification

Hotels in the Netherlands are classified under the Benelux Hotel Classification scheme which also operates in the neighbouring countries of Luxembourg and Belgium. All properties are inspected every two years to ensure that standards are met. The system places strong emphasis on safety and hotels failing to make the grade are declassified. A shield denoting the rating of each hotel is displayed prominently near the main entrance.

Bilderberg Garden Hotel (Map B–C5)

This is a bright, modern hotel, smaller than most in the five-star bracket, with 98 rooms and a haute cuisine French restaurant, the Mangerie de Kersentuin.

✉ *Dijsselhof-plantsoen 7*
☎ *020 664 2220*
📠 *020 679 9356*

Hilton Amsterdam

(Map B–C5)
This canalside luxury hotel has its own marina and a fleet of boats for hire.
✉ *Apollolaan 138–140*
☎ *020 710 6000*
📠 *020 710 9000*

Holiday Inn Amsterdam

(Map B–F6)
De luxe international chain museum situated opposite the Amstelpark and only 500m away from the RAI exhibition and congress centre.
✉ *De Boelelaan 2*
☎ *020 646 2300*
📠 *020 646 4790*

Amsterdam Marriott Hotel

(Map A–A6)
Next to Vondelpark and Leidseplein, handy for museums and the city centre.
✉ *Stadhouders-kade 12*
☎ *020 607 5555*
📠 *020 607 5511*

Hotel Okura Amsterdam

(Map B–E4)
Functional but convenient five-star, five minutes walk from the RAI centre. Facilities include four restaurants, two of them Japanese.
✉ *Ferdinand Bolstraat 333*
☎ *020 678 7111*
📠 *020 671 2344*

Hotel Apollo First

(Map B–C5)
Elegant, small family-owned hotel.
✉ *Apollolaan 123*
☎ *020 673 0333*
📠 *020 675 0348*

Parkhotel

(Map A–B6)
This comfortable four-star is situated around

the corner from the Van Gogh Museum and the Rijksmuseum.
✉ *Stadhouderskade 25,* ☎ *020 671 1222*
✆ *020 664 9455*

- **MID-RANGE**
Toro Hotel
(Map B–B4)
Housed in two pretty turn-of-the-century homes, this small 22-room hotel is decorated with antiques. Located on the edge of the Vondelpark, overlooking the lake.
✉ *Koningslaan 64, 1075 AG Amsterdam*
☎ *020 673 7223*
✆ *020 675 0031*

Schiphol Airport

All airport hotels provide a free shuttle bus service to and from the airport terminal. There is no budget accommodation at the airport.

- **LUXURY**
Golden Tulip Hotel Barbizon Schiphol
(Map I–D3)
This conveniently located luxury hotel is

situated close to the airport terminal.
✉ *Kruisweg 495*
☎ *020 655 0500*
✆ *020 653 4999*

Amsterdam Schiphol Airport Hilton (Map I–D3)
Located in the airport complex, just two minutes from the terminal by shuttle.
✉ *Herbergierstraat 1*
☎ *020 603 4567*
✆ *020 603 4781*

Crowne Plaza Amsterdam-Schiphol (Map I–D3)
This is another luxury hotel, located just 2km (1¼ miles) from the airport.
✉ *Planeetbaan 2, Hoofddorp*
☎ *023 565 0000*
✆ *023 565 0521*

- **MID-RANGE**
Hotel Mercure Schiphol Terminal
(Map I–D3)
This is the only hotel that is actually inside the terminal. It is accessible from the arrivals level in the south lounge and

from the upper floor west lounge.
✉ *Schiphol Airport*
☎ *020 604 1339*
✆ *020 615 9027*

Dorint Hotel Schiphol Amsterdam (Map I–D2)
This four-star hotel is situated midway between the airport and central Amsterdam. There is a free shuttle bus to the terminal every 20 minutes.
✉ *Sloterweg 299*
☎ *020 658 8288*
✆ *020 659 7101*

Camp Sites
Camping Vliegenbos (Map I–E2)
Across the IJ in north Amsterdam, 10 minutes from the centre by ferry, this well-appointed camp site has its own shop and restaurant, washing machines and driers, and accommodation in hiker's cabins for those without tents.
✉ *Meeuwenlaan 138*
☎ *020 636 8855*
✆ *020 632 2723*
🕑 *open from 1 Apr to 30 Sep*

EATING OUT

Above: *A range of Dutch cheeses.*
Opposite: *Open-air cafés abound and are an attractive part of Amsterdam's summer scene.*

Food and Drink

Dutch cooking retains its country roots. Traditional Dutch cooks favour big portions simply cooked and accompanied by plenty of carbohydrates – food created to stick to the ribs of hungry farmers, dockers and fishermen, rather than for the waistline-conscious visitor.

A typical Dutch breakfast comprises bread with jam, honey or other sweet spreads, plenty of cheese, sliced sausage or cold meat (usually ham), and lashings of coffee. Lunch for most Amsterdam workers is a light snack or buffet, not very different from breakfast. The main hot meal of the day in most households is eaten early in the evening and made up of three courses – soup or some other starter, a substantial main course of vegetables, meat and potatoes, often in the form of a stew or casserole, and a sweet dessert. Though many restaurants specializing in Dutch cuisine stay open until later in the evening, reflecting a trend away from early dining, many of the older-fashioned small Dutch restaurants tend to close at 20:00.

Restaurants in Amsterdam offer a host of different eating experiences, from exotic Indonesian, Thai and Chinese to spicy Turkish. Also available are Italian, Greek, Tex-Mex and French. Among the exciting newer trends are the festive Spanish-style tapas restaurants as well as Japanese sushi bars.

Fast food ranges from hamburgers or felafel to shish kebab, pizza, and fish and chips. Amsterdam also has its very own home-grown fast food. Pastry shops sell not only delicious sweet pies and pastries but tasty savouries. Butchers' shops frequently sell freshly baked rolls filled with an assortment of cold meats or meat balls, while fishmongers sell bite-sized morsels of fried fish, smoked eel, smoked salmon or shellfish.

But the snack which typifies Amsterdam is **herring**, bought from a fishmonger or from a herring stall. These are dotted all over the city centre, especially in the areas

Say Cheese
The **Waag** (Weigh-house) in **Gouda** (*see page 83*) is the symbol of a town associated in so many visitors' minds with fine Dutch cheese. Built by the architect Pieter Post in 1668, it is still the centre of the weekly summer cheese market, when dairy farmers from the surrounding countryside bring their great rounds of yellow cheese to the Markt (market square) to be weighed and sold. Above the entrance a stone relief depicts a pair of giant scales, the emblem of the cheesemakers' guild. If you're there on a Thursday in summer, when the cheeses are being weighed, you will not be allowed to leave without sampling a slice of cheese.

Geniever

Geniever, Amsterdam's traditional spirit, is similar to gin but much more strongly flavoured. It gets its name from *ginebra*, the Spanish word for juniper, which is its main flavouring, but other herbs such as caraway and coriander can also go into the mix. Locals use lots of slang terms for a shot of geniever and the beer chaser which often goes with it. Ask for a *borrel*, a *hasse-bassie*, *keiltje*, *neutje*, *pikketanussie*, a *recht op en neer* or a *slokkie* – the barman will know what you mean. A beer chaser is a *kopstoot* (knock on the head), a *kabouter pils* (dwarf pils) or *lampie licht* (little lamp), and a large glass of ale a *bakkie* (jar) or a *vaas* (vase).

Below: *Heineken, exported all over the world, is Amsterdam's most famous beer.*

around the market streets. Chopped bits of raw herring are served with chopped onion or pepper and eaten with a cocktail stick.

Vegetarians, **vegans** and other travellers who require special diets will find that central Amsterdam offers as wide a choice of places to eat as anywhere in Europe. The city's role as a counter-culture capital spawned many 'alternative' eating places, especially in the still faintly bohemian Jordaan area. Though the Jewish community is now only a remnant, the city's Jewish heritage is carried on in a handful of good kosher restaurants, snack bars, bakeries and delicatessen. The presence of substantial Indonesian, Turkish and Middle Eastern communities means there are also numerous eating places catering for Muslim tastes.

Alcohol, coffee and tobacco have important roles to play in the social life of the city. Dutch **coffee**, a taste developed over five centuries, is excellent and is served in bars and cafés. Dutch **beers**, notably Heineken, Amstel and Grolsch, enjoy a worldwide reputation. Beer is served on draught – in small glasses with a disproportionately large head of foam – or in bottles. Amsterdam's native spirit is **geniever**. This highly alcoholic, strongly flavoured beverage is drunk neat and is an acquired taste. Throughout the city centre, you will find bars serving a wide range of imported beers, wines and spirits as well as local products. The

Netherlands is not traditionally a wine-drinking country, and though imported wines are widely available, quality is not always high and prices are much higher than in Europe's wine-producing countries.

Above: *There's always somewhere to take the weight off your feet.*

Where to Eat

Amsterdam has a tremendous choice of places to eat, most of them concentrated in the city centre. Every cuisine in the world is represented. Restaurants found around the Leidseplein and Rembrandtplein areas tend to be very touristy, with prices and menus to match. Cheaper places to eat, many of them offering Middle Eastern, Greek, Indonesian or Turkish menus, can be found around the Nieuwendijk and Zeedijk near Centraal Station. Several small, pleasant restaurants with an affordable menu and a faintly bohemian air are scattered around the Jordaan district.

For those on a tight budget, there are also plenty of snack bars selling burgers, kebabs, chips, felafel and other cheap and filling snacks on these streets. Many of the city's finest restaurants are in its top city-centre hotels.

Brown Cafés

Brown cafés – so called because the smoke from centuries of pipes, cigars and cigarettes has kippered walls and ceilings to a rich tan colour – are an Amsterdam institution. Many started life as *proeflokalen* (tasting houses) where potential customers could sample a glass of geniever before buying in quantity. In those days quality control was less thorough than it is now, and each batch of geniever might be different from the last, so customers expected a free sample. These days, you have to pay for your taste in the city's surviving *proeflokalen*.

City Centre

• LUXURY
De Poort
This fine old Dutch restaurant is noted for its steaks.
⊠ Hotel die Port van Cleve, Nieuwezijds Voorburgwal 176–180
☎ 020 624 4860
📞 020 622 0240

Café Roux
Excellent Roux Brothers restaurant, open for lunch and dinner.
⊠ Grand Hotel, Oudezijds Voorburgwal 197
☎ 020 555 3111
📞 020 555 3222

De Goudsbloem
Fine small hotel restaurant; with the emphasis on French cooking. It boasts Amsterdam's longest wine list.
⊠ Pulitzer Hotel, Prinsengracht 315-331
☎ 020 523 5235
📞 020 627 6753

Christophe
French restaurant with one Michelin star, probably the best in Amsterdam. Open for dinner only, booking is essential.
⊠ Leliegracht 46
☎ 020 625 0807

De Trechter
French restaurant with one Michelin star. Dinner only.
⊠ Hobbemakade 63
☎ 020 671 1263

't Swarte Schaep
Just off the Leidseplein. Hearty Dutch meals served; go for the 17th-century interior as much as for the food.
⊠ Korte Leidsedwarsstraat 24
☎ 020 622 3021

D'Vijff Vlieghen
The most famous and the best of Amsterdam's Dutch restaurants. Lots of tiny rooms in 17th-century building.
⊠ Spuistraat 294
☎ 020 624 8369

De Oesterbar
Up-market seafood restaurant.
⊠ Leidseplein 10
☎ 020 623 2988

Les Quatre Canetons

Good quality French restaurant.

✉ *Prinsengracht 1111*

☎ *020 624 6307*

• *MID-RANGE*
New Bali

This is Amsterdam's best Indonesian restaurant. The enormous *rijstaffel* of about 20 different dishes is real value for money.

✉ *Leidsestraat 95*

☎ *020 622 7878*

✆ *020 626 2465*

't Haringhuis

This is the best place in town to try tradi-tional Dutch herring and other tasty seafood dishes.

✉ *Oude Doelenstraat 18,* ☎ *020 622 1284*

Tapasbar A la Plancha

This is a cheerful, affordable Spanish restaurant offering tapas dishes and wines by the glass.

✉ *1e Looierdwars-straat 15*

☎ *020 420 3633*

Zushi

One of the new trendy sushi bars in Amsterdam, with automat price-coded service.

✉ *Amstel 20*

☎ *020 330 6882*

In de Waag

International cuisine is on the menu in this café-restaurant located inside the old 15th-century city gate.

✉ *Nieuwmarkt 4*

☎ *020 422 7772*

Below: *Brown cafés like this one are, sadly, increasingly rare on Amsterdam's street corners.*

Sea Palace

Near Centraal Station, this vast, Hong Kong-style floating restaurant has a fine view of the Oosterdok and the IJ.

✉ Oosterdokskade 8
☎ 020 626 4777

Haesje Claes

Affordable restaurant, specializing in Dutch regional dishes.

✉ Spuistraat 273
☎ 020 624 9998

Below: *People relaxing outside one of the city's euphemistically named 'coffee shops'.*

• BUDGET

Soup en zo

Soup and snack restaurant which also serves freshly squeezed juices.

✉ Jodenbreestraat 94a, ☎ 020 422 2243

Sap & Soup

The name means 'juice and soup' and that is what this outfit serves.

✉ Haarlemmerstraat 68, ☎ 020 320 9190

Turkiye

Good value-for-money Turkish restaurant.

✉ Nieuwezijds Voorburgwal 169
☎ 020 622 9919

Sal Meijer Sandwichshop

Serves kosher sandwiches to eat in or take away.

✉ Scheldestraat 45
☎ 020 673 1313

Eten and Drinken

This is probably the best bargain in town. It is open almost around the clock, with a dish of the

day served with generous helpings of fries and salad.
⊠ *Warmoesstraat 7*

Oibibio

Bright, cheerful, affordable vegetarian café-restaurant.
⊠ *Prins Hendrikkade 20–21*
☎ *020 553 9355*

Traditional Taverns
Café Chris

Old tavern dating from 1624. Builders working on the nearby Westerkerk are said to have received their wages here.
⊠ *Bloemstraat 42*
☎ *020 624 5942*

Café Karpershoek

Opened in 1629 and still more popular with locals than visitors. Sit outside for a view of the station and the Open Haven. Opens at 07:00, so it's a good place for an early morning coffee if you have an early train to catch.
⊠ *Martelaarsgracht 2,*
☎ *020 624 7886*

Café de Druif

Claimed to have been here since 1631 and to have been a favourite drinking place of legendary naval hero Piet Heyn; however, as Heyn died in 1629, this tradition does not bear up under close scrutiny.
⊠ *Rapenburg 83*
☎ *020 624 4530*

Café Papeneiland

This restaurant opened in 1642 on the edge of the Jordaan, beside the Brouwersgracht. The exterior has beautiful step gables.
⊠ *Prinsengracht 2*
☎ *020 624 1989*

De Drie Fleschjes

Opened in 1650, this café has been the tasting-house for Hendrik Bootz liqueurs since 1816.
⊠ *Gravenstraat 18*
☎ *020 624 8443*

Café Hoppe

A very popular old café in the heart of the city, whose clientele often spills

'Coffee Shops'

Amsterdam has long had a liberal attitude towards soft drug use. Possession of cannabis resin (hash) or marijuana (grass) is not legal but the authorities long ago gave up prosecuting discreet users. In euphemistically named 'coffee shops' customers can choose any of a dozen types of mind-expanding substances to enjoy at home or over a cup of coffee on the premises. There are about 450 'coffee shops' in Amsterdam, 180 of them in the inner city. As a result of this policy, cannabis users are less likely to come into contact with hard drugs, and the Netherlands has a much lower rate of hard drug addiction than many other countries with much tougher regimes.

Above: *Amsterdam has bars, pubs and cafés to suit all tastes, all budgets and all age groups.*

out onto the street outside during the summer months.
⊠ *Spui 18–20*
☎ *020 624 7849*

Café Kalkhoven

Facing the Westerkerk, this café may have been open as long ago as 1630, making it the fourth oldest tavern in the city.
⊠ *Prinsengracht 283*
☎ *020 624 9649*

Wijnand Fockink

The inside of this tasting-house, which dates from as long ago as 1679, is decorated with an interesting collection of geniever bottles painted with the portraits of every mayor of the city since 1591.
⊠ *Pijlsteeg 31*
☎ *020 639 2695*

Café In de Wildeman

Founded in 1690, this popular café offers patrons a range of 150 beers from all over the world. Unlike most of the taverns in Amsterdam, it also offers a non-smoking room.
⊠ *Dam 11*
☎ *020 623 0815*

Café 't Smalle

Restored to its original 18th-century condition about 20 years ago, this is one of the finest old-fashioned cafés in the city.
⊠ *Egelantiersgracht 12,* ☎ *020 623 9617*

Outside the Centre

The area to the south and west of the

Singelgracht and east of the River Amstel is a diner's desert, where restaurants, except for those in large hotels, are thin on the ground.

• *LUXURY*

Sazanka Teppan Yaki and **Yamazoto**
Fine Japanese dining.
✉ *Hotel Okura, Ferdinand Bolstraat 333*
☎ *020 678 7111*
🖶 *020 671 2344*

Le Ciel Bleu
French haute cuisine.
✉ *Hotel Okura, Ferdinand Bolstraat 333*
☎ *020 678 7111*
🖶 *020 671 2344*

Gambrinus
This French restaurant is rather expensive.
✉ *Ferdinand Bolstraat 80*
☎ *020 671 7389*

Chambertin
Stylish fin-de-siècle restaurant with an attractive garden.
✉ *Hotel Apollo First, Apollolaan 123*
☎ *020 673 0333*
🖶 *020 675 0348*

• *MID-RANGE*

Ambrosia
Caribbean-style restaurant where prices are reasonable.
✉ *Stadhouderskade 31,* ☎ *020 664 0408*

Below: *Old-fashioned pubs like this one attract regulars looking for a quiet drink and a chat.*

Above: *The bright lights of the red-light district reflected from an Amsterdam canal.*

ENTERTAINMENT
Nightlife

Amsterdam is well-known as one of Europe's liveliest after-dark cities, with a choice of entertainment out of all proportion to its size, spanning everything from high culture to lowlife. Whether your tastes include opera, cinema, theatre, ballet, jazz, rock, blues, dance, trance or striptease, Amsterdam is able to pander to them every night of the week and virtually around the clock.

Cinema

English-speaking cinema-goers are also in for a treat in Amsterdam, as almost all English-language films are shown un-dubbed (with Dutch subtitles) in the city's dozens of cinemas.

Casino
If gambling is your thing, head for the **Holland Casino Amsterdam**, ✉ 64 Max Euweplein, ☎ 020 620 1006. Games available for punters include roulette, blackjack, poker and a wide variety of electronic gambling machines.

The eccentric **Pathe Tuschinski Cinema** stands out from the rather undistinguished postwar buildings situated around it. Built in 1921 by Abraham Tuschinksi, its Art Deco exterior of glossy dark brick looks like the castle of some sorceror, while the foyer is a lavish kitsch fantasy of coloured marble, mosaics and brass chandeliers. It still functions as a cinema and is open daily. With its six screens, it has the widest choice of English-language screenings available in Amsterdam.

Other cinemas in Amsterdam include the **City Cinema**, with seven screens. For up-to-date weekly listings of what's on at all Amsterdam's many cinemas, pick up a copy of the free film magazine *Film Agenda* (in English) which is available at cinemas, most hotels, and many cafés.

Theatre

Just south of the Magere Brug, on the east bank of the Amstel, is an imposing, domed building. This is the **Theatre Carré**, built in 1887 by the impresario Oscar Carré to house his permanent circus. The circus did not survive its founder and since the beginning of the 20th century it has been a venue for opera and operetta.

The **Melkweg** is a bunker-like brick building on the Lijnbaangracht canal. It was originally a dairy and is now a time-honoured survivor of the 1960s and early 1970s when Amsterdam established itself as the counter-culture capital of Europe. It was the venue for countless happenings and free concerts and is now an avant-garde venue for all sorts of experimental performance and high-tech art.

Cinemas
Pathe Tuschinski Cinema
✉ Reguliersbreestraat 26
☎ 020 626 2633
🚋 Tram 4, 9, 14

City Cinema
✉ Kleine Gartman-plantsoen 15–19
☎ 020 623 4579
🚋 Tram 1, 2, 5, 6, 7, 10

Theatre Carré
✉ Amstel 115–125
☎ 0900 25 25 255
Ⓜ Amstel

Melkweg
✉ Lijnbaansgracht 234A
☎ 020 531 8181
🚋 Tram 1, 2, 5, 6, 7, 10

Bellevue Cinerama
✉ Marnixstraat 400
☎ 0623 4876

Cinecenter
✉ Lijnbaansgracht 236
☎ 0623 6615
🚋 Tram 1, 2, 5, 6, 7, 10

Cinema de Balle
✉ Kleine Gartmans-plantsoen 13–25
☎ 020 553 5100
🚋 Tram 1, 2, 5, 6, 7, 10

Pathe de Munt
✉ Vijzelstraat 15
☎ 0900 1458
🚋 Tram 4, 9, 14, 16, 24, 15

Beurs van Berlage
✉ Beursplein
☎ 020 530 4141

Concertgebouw
✉ 2–6 Concert-
gebouwplein
☎ 020 671 8345
🕐 12:30 Wed (free
lunchtime concerts)

Muziektheater
✉ Amstel 3
☎ 020 625 5455
🕐 box office open
10:00 until perform-
ance Mon–Sat, 11:30
until performance Sun

Stadsschouwburg
✉ Leidseplein 26
☎ 020 624 2311

Below: *The
Concertgebouw has
changed the cultural
face of the city.*

Conference Centre

Amsterdam's main conference and exhibion centre, the **RAI Congresgebouw**, occupies a site on the edge of Nieuw Zuid. It has its own metro light rail station and is the venue, each June, for **Kunst RAI**, an important exhibition of contemporary art.

Classical Music and Opera

The Netherlands has produced no instantly recognized great composer, but its performing musicians are highly regarded worldwide. The city's **Royal Concertgebouw Orchestra** has come a long way since Johannes Brahms, visiting the city for a performance of his work in 1876, described the Dutch as 'wonderful people but dreadful musicians.' The **Concertgebouw**, built in 1888 by a group of businessmen determined to improve the city's philistine reputation, was restored and extended between 1985 and 1988, giving the orchestra a vastly improved venue. Its acoustics

Above: *The Beurs van Berlage building is an early 20th-century architectural classic.*

are reputed to be among the finest in the world, and the Royal Concertgebouw Orchestra is claimed to be among the five greatest orchestras in the world.

Both the **Nederlandse Opera** and the **Nationale Ballet** are now housed in the **Musiktheater** complex, overlooking the Amstel River. Seating just under 1700 people in its vast auditorium, this sprawling complex of modern glass and concrete buildings is familiarly known as the **Stopera**. The theatre, opened amid much controversy in 1986, gave the two companies a more appropriate home after many years of having to make do with old-fashioned and outmoded venues.

Midway along the Damrak, Beursplein is dominated on its north and east sides by the buildings of the **Beurs van Berlage** and the Effectenbeurs. Built in 1903 and named after its architect, Hendrik Petrus Berlage, a pupil of Cuypers, the spare lines and elegant proportions of the Beurs (or Exchange) make it a classic of early 20th-

Beurs Clock Tower
The clock tower of the **Beurs van Berlage** bears the motto *Beidt uw tijd* (Bide your time). This is appropriate enough, considering that Berlage was only a runner-up in the first competition to appoint an architect for the building. He won a second contest after the winner of the first was found to have pirated his design from another building.

century architecture. The Beurs has been a concert hall since 1988 and is now home to the **Netherlands Philharmonic Orchestra**. Its former commercial activities have been transferred to the neighbouring Effectenbeurs (Commodities Exchange), located on the eastern side of the square.

The world-famous **Concertgebouw** is the main venue for classical orchestral music performed by world-class musicians; the **Muziektheater** presents classical music, opera and ballet, while the **Stadsschouwburg** is a grand venue for classical music performances.

Above: *Amsterdam's street musicians keep visitors and locals entertained year-round.*
Opposite: *Strip clubs line the Oudezijds Voorburgwal in the Walletjes, Amsterdam's sleazy red-light district.*

The Concertgebouw, the Muziektheater, the Stadsschouwburg and the Beurs van Berlage are on the international circuit for the world's leading orchestras and theatre companies. Rather than calling individual theatre box offices, make your bookings through **VVV tourist offices** or through the **AUB Ticket Shop** (personal callers only) or by telephone through the **AUB Uitlijn**.

Rock, Jazz and Blues

Tourist nightlife centres around the Leidseplein, Rembrandtsplein and surrounding streets, where virtually every bar and café plays live music (anything from rock to

AUB Ticket Shop
✉ Leidseplein 26
🕐 10:00–18:00 Mon–Sat, until 21:00 Thu

AUB Uitlijn
☎ 020 621 1211

blues or jazz) after dark. Admission is free to most of these establishments, but drinks are more expensive than in bars which don't offer live music. Amsterdam has far too many bars offering live music nightly to list exhaustively, but some recommended venues around the city include:

Pianobar le Maxim, ✉ Leidsekruisstraat 35, ☎ 020 624 1920. Easy-listening piano music, cocktail bar ambience.

Ciel Bleu Bar, ✉ Okura Hotel, Ferdinand Bolstraat 175, ☎ 020 678 7111. One of the city's better hotel cocktail bars.

Bamboo Bar, ✉ Lange Leidsedwarsstraat 66, ☎ 020 624 3993. Jazz and blues live.

Joseph Lam Jazz Café, ✉ van Diemenstraat 242, ☎ 020 622 3626. Specializes in Dixieland jazz, Fri–Sun night only.

Melkweg, ✉ Lijnbaansgracht 234A, ☎ 020 624 1777. Venerable alternative music and performance venue founded in the 1960s and still going strong.

Harbour Ferries
The cheapest excursion in the city, and the best viewpoint from which to enjoy a vista of the harbour, the IJ and the city waterfront, is the free ferry trip that runs from the Pont naar Tolhuis piers behind Centraal Station to the north side of the IJ. The trip offers a fine view of the harbour and its busy shipping, including the stubby barges from the river and canal ports of Germany and the Netherlands and giant container ships like walls of rusty steel. There is no better symbol of the relationship between Amsterdam and the sea; the two vast harbour basins and the dock islands with their 40km (25 miles) of quayside are entirely man-made.

Striptease

Amsterdam's red-light district offers its own brand of nightlife. One of the places you could go to is **Casa Rosso**, ✉ Oudezijds Voorburgwal 106–108, ☎ 020 627 8954, which tries to present erotica as good clean fun; at least they don't water the drinks and your wallet should be safe.

Gay and Lesbian Clubs

Amsterdam has a thriving gay nightlife scene. Venues, as ever, go in and out of fashion but there are lots of gay clubs in the Rembrandtsplein area. Look at *Time Out: Amsterdam*, the monthly listings magazine, for the latest places to go.

Discos and Dance Clubs

Discos and dance clubs in Amsterdam cater to all tastes, from middle-aged, middle-of-the-road disco music to the latest in trance and techno. In keeping with the city's long-standing egalitarian culture, door policies and dress codes tend to be much more relaxed than in bigger, more style conscious cities such as London and New York, and most venues attract a much more mixed audience – in terms of age and gender preference – than clubs elsewhere in Europe. In that sense, the city's nightlife scene is a microscosm of the cosmopolitan world outside the club doors. Amsterdam's two landmark venues, Paradiso and Melkweg, both have their roots in the heady days of the underground drug and music culture of the 1960s and 1970s, and there's still a faint whiff of the anything-goes idealism of that era.

While not yet on a par with London or Ibiza, Amsterdam has a lively enough dance music scene to satisfy the most discerning clubber, from giant venues like the recently expanded Move and the vast Power Zone to smaller, more intimate and relaxed venues. The city's thriving gay scene centres on Rembrandtplein, with gay bars and clubs also around Kerkstraat, Warmoesstraat and Reguliersdwarsstraat.

Move

The latest disco, Move, is in the former Roothanhuis building. Gay nights Wed, garage and two-step Fri, DJs and other club nights through the week.
✉ *Rozengracht 133*

Club Panama

In a restored 19th-century warehouse. Live concerts as well as a range of different music and DJs in different rooms.
✉ *corner of Oostelijke Handelskade and Veemkade*

Paradiso

Contact VVV Amsterdam Tourist Office for Paradiso's programme and tickets. This mecca of modern music is housed in a former church. Fantastic acoustics, the best atmosphere in the city, one of the coolest places in Europe for 30 years. Best live music and dance nights in town. **VIP Club** on Fri for techno, drum & bass, big beat and speed-garage. **Paradisco**, twice monthly on Sat, for soul, funk, disco. **Bassline,** twice a month on Sun, for hip-hop.
✉ *6–8 Weteringschans, Leidseplein*

Arena Club

Full-service budget hotel (Europe's largest), café-restaurant and all-night party club. For tickets and information, contact VVV Amsterdam Tourist Office.
✉ *'s Gravesandstraat 51*

Jazz Café Alto

This is a legendary jazz bar, with a central location just off Leidseplein, and a slightly more mature audience. Expect quality music in a pleasant and informal atmosphere.
✉ *Korte Leidsedwarsstraat 115*
☎ *020 626 3249*
🕐 *21:00–05:00*

Odeon

Housed in one of the city's oldest music venues, Odeon is chic but not too style-conscious; balcony bar above the dance floor and a playlist of funky tunes attracting the 20–30 age group.
✉ *Singel 460*
☎ *020 624 9711*
🕐 *Sun–Wed 11:00–03:00, Thu 11:00–04:00, Fri–Sat 11:00–05:00*

Club Zyon

Big dance floor with lots of chill-out space, space-age décor and DJs playing a large list of house, techno, R&B, trance and hip-hop.
✉ *Nieuwezijds Voorburgwal 161*
☎ *020 427 5961*
🕐 *Thu–Sun 11:00–04:00*

Power Zone

Amsterdam's biggest club (room for more than 5000 dancers) is outside the city centre, in the warehouse and industrial area and offers an awesome night out, well worth the short Metro ride to Spaklerweg station.
✉ *Daniel Goedkoopstraat 1-3*
☎ *020 681 88 66*
✉ *Fri–Sat 11:00–05:00*

EXCURSIONS

Within a 60km (37-mile) radius of Amsterdam lie the Randstad towns. An excellent road and rail network means that all are less than 45 minutes away from Amsterdam, and many of them repay an excursion from the city.

Above: *The Binnenhof in The Hague, seat of princes and politicians.*
Opposite: *Blue and white chinaware, a souvenir of Delft.*

The Hague
Location: Map F
Distance from Amsterdam: 56km (45 miles)

The Binnenhof
✉ Binnenhof 8A
☎ 070 364 6144
🕐 10:00–16:00 Mon–Sat

Mauritshuis
✉ Korte Vijverberg 8
☎ 070 302 3435
🕐 10:00–17:00 Tue–Sat, 11:00–17:00 Sun
💰 15 Euros

Gevangenpoort Museum
✉ Buitenhof 33
☎ 070 346 0861
🕐 10:00–16:00 Tue–Fri, 13:00–17:00 Sat–Sun
💰 3.60 Euros

The Hague

Den Haag (The Hague) has been the capital of the Netherlands since the 16th century. The oldest part of the splendid **Binnenhof** complex is its 13th-century castle. Within, the **Ridderzaal** (Knights' Hall) is used for the ceremonial opening of Parliament each September. The newer wing, built in 1913, houses the ministry of public affairs and incorporates an octagonal 15th-century turret, now the Prime Minister's office.

Just west of the Binnenhof is the **Grote Kerk** (St Jacob's Church). Rebuilt after a fire in 1539, the church is still a treasury of 16th-century craftsmanship. The pulpit dates from 1550, and two richly stained glass windows are attributed to the mid-16th century artist Dirk Crabeth.

The Hague has several museums. The most famous is **Mauritshuis**, home to the Royal Collection of Paintings. This is one of the finest collections of old Dutch masters, and includes the world's largest collection of Rembrandts. The **Gevangenpoort** (Prison Gate) **Museum** was used as a jail by the Counts of Holland from about 1420. It is now a national museum exhibiting grisly instruments of torture. **Museum Bredius** has a fine collection of works by Rembrandt, Cuyp and Van der Neer in a fine Rococo interior. The **Lange Voorhout Palace Museum** was a royal residence from 1845, and is now a museum with a changing programme of art and historic exhibitions. Napoleon spent a night here in 1811.

Top attractions of The Hague include the **Panorama Mesdag**, an amazing panoramic painting of the seaside at Scheveningen. Painted by Hendrik Willem Mesdag (1831–1915), his wife and some friends, it is one of the largest paintings in the world. Don't miss the **Mesdag Museum**, a fine collection of 19th-century Dutch and French paintings, and **Madurodam**, an open-air reconstruction of Dutch towns in miniature. It is very popular with children.

Delft

Among the prettiest towns in the Netherlands, Delft's narrow canals are lined with trees and criss-crossed by wrought-iron footbridges. Most landmarks date from the 16th century.

Het Prinsenhof (Prince's Court) was the headquarters of William the Silent during his struggle with Spain. It is now a museum devoted to the history of the Dutch Republic. In the Moordhal ('Murder Hall'), where William was assassinated in 1584 by the fanatic Balthazar Gerard, you can see two holes said to have been made by the assassin's bullets.

Museum Bredius
✉ Lange Vijverberg 14
☎ 070 362 0729
🕐 12:00–17:00 Tue–Sun
💰 4.50 Euros

Lange Voorhout Palace Museum
✉ Lange Voorhout 74
☎ 070 338 1111
🕐 10:00–17:00 Tue–Sat, 11:00–17:00 Sun
💰 8 Euros

Panorama Mesdag
✉ Zeestraat 65
☎ 070 364 4544
🕐 10:00–17:00 Mon–Sat, 12:00–17:00 Sun
💰 5 Euros

Mesdag Museum
✉ Laan van der Meerderfoort 7F
☎ 070 362 1434
🕐 12:00–17:00 Tue–Sun
💰 7 Euros

Madurodam
✉ George Maduroplein 1
☎ 070 416 2400
🕐 daily 09:00–22:30 Mar–May, 09:00–23:00 Jun–Aug, 09:00–21:30 Sep, 09:00–18:00 Oct–Dec

Delft
Location: Map G
Distance from
Amsterdam: 64km
(40 miles)

Tourist Office
✉ Hippolytusbuurt 4
☎ 015 215 4051
🖥 www.delft.nl

Museum Lambert
van Meerten
✉ Oude Delft
☎ 015 260 2538
🕐 10:00–17:00 Tue–
Sat, 13:00–17:00 Sun

Museum Tetar van
Elven
✉ Koornemarkt
☎ 015 212 4206
🕐 13:00–17:00 Tue–
Sun (Apr–Oct)

Armamentarium
✉ Korte Geer 1
☎ 015 215 0500
🕐 10:00–17:00
Tue–Fri, 12:00–17:00
Sat–Sun

Below: *There are*
fantastic views of
Rotterdam and its
harbours from the
top of the Euromast.

Delft has some interesting museums. The **Museum Lambert van Meerten** displays a collection of hundreds of 17th- and 18th-century Delft tiles. The **Museum Tetar van Elven** is named after a 19th-century imitator of Vermeer, who left his 18th-century mansion to the nation with its period furniture, Delftware and paintings. The 17th-century armoury houses the **Armamentarium** (Delft Military Museum), exhibiting Dutch military history, maps and weapons.

Rotterdam

Rotterdam has been an important seaport for more than two centuries, and the sea and the city's seafaring connections are well represented in its maritime museums.

The richest exhibits in the **Prince Hendrik Maritime Museum** are in the Treasure House: trophies and booty brought home by Dutch adventurers of the Golden Age. Moored outside the museum is the restored 19th-century steam cruiser *Buffel*.

The Leuvenhaven's west quay is a clutter of maritime equipment, forming the collection of the **Open Air Maritime Museum**. A fleet of Dutch sailing barges forms the collection of the **Openlucht Binnenvaart Museum** (the Open-Air Inland Navigation Museum). The **Mariniers Museum der Koninklijke Marine** (Royal Marine Corps Museum) is a collection devoted to the Dutch Marine Corps. The Dutch can take credit for commissioning the first such force of seagoing soldiers: the Royal Marine Corps was founded in 1665.

Other museums include the **Museum Boymans-van Beuningen** with works by Brueghel, Bosch, Rembrandt, Da Vinci, Cezanne, Picasso, Dalí, Van Gogh and Appel. Also interesting are the **Museum voor Volkenkunde** (Museum of Ethnology) and **Het Schielandshuis** (Rotterdam History Museum).

Built in 1960, **Euromast** is a vertiginous experience. Take a high-speed lift to the 100m (330ft) high Space Platform. There, sound and lighting effects mimic a real rocket launch and, rotating slowly, you climb into orbit to 185m (610ft).

Above: *Leiden's grand Town Hall dates from Rembrandt's day.*

Leiden

Leiden is the birthplace of Rembrandt and has one of Europe's oldest and most respected universities and some interesting museums. One of the buildings surviving from Rembrandt's day is the **Stadhuis** (Town Hall) in the town centre.

The **Rijksmuseum van Oudenheden** (National Museum of Antiquities) is the finest archaeological museum in the Netherlands, with a collection of mainly Egyptian antiquities. A section devoted to local archaeology gives a complete overview of Dutch history.

The **Stedelijk Museum de Lakenhal** has paintings by Rembrandt's teachers Swanenburg and Lastman and an early work by Rembrandt himself. Lucas van Leyden's *The Last Judgement* (1572) is one of the gems of the collection.

Molen De Valk (Falcon Windmill), a tall, circular brick tower with a gallery just

Rotterdam
Location: Map H
Distance from Amsterdam: 80km
(50 miles)

Tourist Office
☎ 070 361 8888
📠 070 361 7915
🖥 www.denhaag.nl

Leiden
Location: Map D
Distance from Amsterdam: 48km
(30 miles)

Tourist Office
✉ Stationsweg 2d
☎ 0900 222 2333
📠 071 516 1227
🖥 www.holland rijnland.nl

below sail-level, is a grain mill that was built in 1743. All seven floors are open, with different displays on each.

Haarlem

Haarlem's most prominent building is **Sint Bavo Kerk** (St Bavo's Church). Built between 1370 and 1520, it is a late Gothic cruciform basilica with a slender wooden tower. The interior is dominated by a splendid organ, ornamented in gilt and crimson and built by the famous Amsterdam organ-maker Christian Muller in 1738. With its 64 registers and 5000 pipes, it is one of the largest church organs in the world. Among its many admirers were Handel and the young Mozart, who played here during his tour of the Low Countries in 1766.

The **Frans Hals Museum** has more than 20 paintings by Hals, which are grouped in the Frans Hals Room. Other 16th- and 17th-century masterpieces include works by Floris van Dijck, Jan Mostaert, Hendrick Cornelisz and Jan van Scorel. There is also an extensive modern collection, and the Restoration Workshop allows visitors to see the painstaking work involved in restoring an old masterpiece to pristine condition.

Utrecht

The **Domkerk** is one of the main attractions of Utrecht. Its tower, the 14th-century Domtoren, is the highest church tower in the Netherlands. The nearby **Pieterskerk** was consecrated in 1048, and is perhaps the oldest in the Netherlands.

Haarlem
Location: Map C
Distance from Amsterdam: 24km
(15 miles)

Tourist Office
✉ Stationsplein 1
☎ 0900 616 1600
📠 023 534 0537
🖥 www.vvvzk.nl

Utrecht
Location: Map E
Distance from Amsterdam: 42km
(26 miles)

Tourist Office
✉ PO Box 3232
☎ 030 296 7777
📠 030 296 6635
🖥 www.utrecht toerisme.nl

The high points of the **Centraal Museum** include a reconstructed Viking ship from around 120AD and a delightful 17th-century doll's house. A room in the museum is devoted to the works of Jan van Scorel, the painter and inventor from Utrecht sometimes called the 'Dutch Leonardo'.

The **Nederlands Spoorwegmuseum** (the Netherlands Railway Museum), housed in the antique Maliebaan station, has over 60 locomotives, carriages and freight wagons.

> **Gouda**
> **Location:** Map J
> **Distance from Amsterdam:** 74km (41 miles)
>
> **Tourist Office**
> ✉ Markt 27
> ☎ 018 251 1300
> 📠 018 258 3210
> 🖥 www.vvvgouda.nl

Gouda

Gouda is everybody's idea of a typical Dutch town. A ring of canals surrounds the pretty 15th-century Gothic town centre. The **Sint Janskerk** is a late Gothic basilica with wooden vaulting, and is noted for its stained-glass windows.

Museums include the **Exposeum Goudse Kaaswaag** (Gouda Cheese Museum), depicting the age-old craft of cheesemaking. The **Stedelijk Museum Het Catharina Gasthuis** (St Catherine's Hospice Museum) has an excellent collection, spanning gruesome surgical instruments, 16th-century altarpieces, and some fine paintings. Also worth a look is the interesting exhibition at the **Zuidhollands Verzetsmuseum** (the South Holland Resistance Museum).

Gouda's **Stadhuis** (Town Hall), built in 1450, it is the oldest free-standing Gothic town hall in the Netherlands.

Opposite: *Haarlem's Sint Bavo Kerk has one of the world's largest organs.*
Below: *Don't leave Gouda without sampling the famous cheese.*

Above: *Amsterdam's tram system is swift, silent and efficient.*

Public Holidays and Festivals
- 1 January – New Year's Day
- March/April (variable) – Good Friday, Easter Sunday and Monday
- April 30 – Queen's Day, celebrating the royal birthday
- 5 May – Liberation Day
- May (variable) – Whit Sunday and Monday, Ascension Day
- 25 December – Christmas Day
- 26 December – Boxing Day.

These are essentially family feast days with generally little public celebration.

Tourist Information

The **Netherlands Board of Tourism** maintains overseas information offices in London, New York, Toronto and Sydney.

VVV Amsterdam Tourist Office has several offices:
- ✉ within Centraal Station (🕘 daily 09:00–17:00);
- ✉ immediately outside Centraal Station at Stationsplein 10 (🕘 daily 08:00–16:00);
- ✉ at Leidseplein 1 (🕘 daily 09:00–19:00);
- ✉ at Stadionplein (🕘 Mon–Sat 09:00–17:00). For **central information:**
- ☎ 0900 400 4040
- 📱 020 625 2869

🕘 daily 09:00–17:00. Other tourist offices include:

VVV Den Haag,
- ✉ Hofweg 1
- ☎ 0900 340 3505
- 📱 0900 352 0426.
- 🖥 www.denhaag.nl

VVV Rotterdam,
- ✉ Coolsingel 67
- ☎ 070 361 8888
- 📱 070 361 7915.

VVV Utrecht,
- ☎ 030 296 7777
- 📱 030 296 6635.

VVV Haarlem,
- ✉ Stationsplein 1
- ☎ 0900 616 1600
- 📱 023 534 0537.

VVV Gouda,
- ✉ Markt 27
- ☎ 018 251 1300
- 📱 018 258 3210.

VVV Leiden,
- ✉ Stationsweg 2d

☎ 0900 222 2333
✆ 071 516 1227.
VVV Delft,
✉ Hippolytusbuurt 4
☎ 015 215 4051
🖥 www.delft.nl
All the VVV offices
in the Randstad
towns have the same
opening times as
those of the Amster-
dam VVV offices.

Entry Requirements

Visas are not required
for citizens of the EU
countries nor for US,
Canadian, Australian,
New Zealand and
South African citizens
intending to stay for a
period of less than
three months.

Customs

Normal European
Union customs
requirements apply.
Those arriving from
outside the EU may
bring in the following
quantities: 200 ciga-
rettes or cigarillos or
50 cigars or 250 grams
of tobacco, 1 litre of
spirits or 2 litres of
wine, 50cc of perfume,
500 grams of coffee or
100 grams of tea.

There are no limits on
the quantities of tax-
paid goods which may
be brough in from or
taken out to other EU
countries for personal
use, but duty-free and
tax-free goods are not
available to those
travelling between EU
countries, including
non-EU nationals.

Health Requirements

None.

Getting There

By air: Amsterdam
Schiphol Airport
(☎ 0900 503 4050) is
15km (9½ miles) from
the city centre and is
connected to the city
by excellent road and
rail links. Trains to
Amsterdam Centraal
Station leave four
times an hour
between 06:00 and
24:00 and hourly
between 01:00 and
05:00; the journey
takes approximately
25 minutes.
Direct trains from
Schiphol also run to
The Hague and to
Rotterdam; the

journey takes less
than an hour.
Schiphol is a major
international airline
hub, with Royal Dutch
Airlines (KLM) and
most other major car-
riers providing service
to cities in North and
South America, Africa,
Asia and Australasia,
and to capitals and
regional hubs
throughout Europe.
By road: Amsterdam
is on the European
motorway network,
with fast highways
connecting it with
other points in the
Netherlands, as well as
Germany to the north
and east, and Belgium
to the south.
By rail: The high-speed
Thalys network, a joint
venture between
Dutch, Belgian and
German railways,
connects Amsterdam
with Cologne and
Düsseldorf in Germany
and with Brussels and
Paris. Thalys trains
connect in Brussels
with high-speed
Eurostar services from
London via the
Channel Tunnel.

By boat: Ferry services connect Hoek van Holland, 90 minutes from Amsterdam by rail or two hours by road, with English North Sea ports including Sheerness and Harwich.

What to Pack

Everyday wear will depend on the season. Comfortable walking footwear, a showerproof coat or jacket, a light sweater and a hat or umbrella are useful even in summer. From September until the end of April be pre-pared for cold, wet weather with sub-zero temperatures, snow and ice from November to March.

Money Matters

The Netherlands is among the European Union states which adopted the single European currency, the euro, in 2002 when the guilder ceased to exist.

Changing money: GWK-Exchange,

✉ Centraal Station
☎ 020 620 8121
🕐 open round the clock every day.
Change Express exchange offices are at ✉ 86 Damrak
☎ 020 624 6682
🕐 08:00–23:45 daily;
✉ 150 Kalverstraat
☎ 020 627 8087
🕐 08:00–20:00 daily;
✉ 1 Leidseplein
☎ 020 622 1425
🕐 08:00–24:00 daily.
There are dozens of other exchange offices throughout the city, many of them charging very high commissions. Check the rate of exchange and the rate of commission before making a transaction.

Travellers cheques: all major travellers cheques and currencies can be exchanged at banks and bureaux de change.

Credit cards: all the major credit cards are widely accepted.

Tipping: it is not essential to tip except in restaurants, where a 15% service charge is normally added to the bill.

Tax: Visitors from outside the European Union can reclaim value added tax on some items that are exported within 30 days of purchase. Many of the shops display a conspicuous 'Tax Free for Tourists' logo and these will be pleased to help you with the tax reclaiming formalities.

Accommodation

Booking a room: the Nederlands Reserverings Centrum (Netherlands Reservation Centre), an organization run by Dutch hotel-owners, handles bookings, free of charge, for around 1700 classified hotels. The NRC works on a service basis, charging no fee to its members or their customers. Booking and confirmation is computerized and you can book by telephone, fax or by mail. The NRC also handles bookings for self-catering apartments and bungalows, as well as for the Holland Festival and other events in Amsterdam. You can contact the **Netherlands Reservation Centre** at ✉ PO Box 404, 2260 AK Leidschendam, Netherlands ☎ 070 419 5500 📠 070 419 5519. Local VVV tourist offices throughout the Netherlands have a national hotel booking system through which you can book a room not only locally but elsewhere in the Netherlands. The only snag is that you have to do it in person: telephone and fax bookings are not allowed. There is a small booking fee. A high-tech Airport Information Panel at Schiphol International Airport arrival hall lists and illustrates hotels with accommodation available, in categories from budget to deluxe, in Amsterdam, Leiden and Utrecht.

Road Signs

Street signs in Holland are in the standardized European format. Many street signs, shop signs and directions are repeated in English. Some useful ones to learn include:

- **Niet roken** – No smoking
- **Gevaar** – Danger
- **Let op** – Look out
- **Pas op** – Beware
- **Toegang verboden** – No entry
- **Vrij toegang** – Free admission
- **Ingang** – Entrance
- **Uitgang** – Exit
- **Open** – Open
- **Gesloten** – Closed

Embassies and Consulates

Some are in Den Haag (The Hague), diplomatic capital of the Netherlands. Dialling code from Amsterdam is 070.
Australia: ✉ 12 Carnegielaan, Den Haag, ☎ 310 8200.
Canada: ✉ 7 Sophialaan, Den Haag, ☎ 361 4111.
Ireland: ✉ Dr Kuyperstraat 9, Den Haag, ☎ 363 0993.
New Zealand: ✉ Mauritskade 25, Den Haag, ☎ 346 9324.
UK: ✉ 44 Koningslaan, Amsterdam, ☎ 676 4343.
USA: ✉ 19 Museumplein, Amsterdam, ☎ 575 5309.

Good Reading
• **Schama, Simon** (1988) *The Embarrassment of Riches.* Harper Collins, London.
• **Gauldie, Robin** (1996) *Walking Amsterdam.* New Holland, London.
• *The Golden Book of Amsterdam* (Bonechi)
• **Bakker, B.** (ed.) (1988) *Amsterdam: The History of the City.* Waanders.
• **Fromentin, Eugène** (1981) *The Masters of Past Time: Dutch and Flemish Painting from Van Eyck to Rembrandt.* Phaidon, London.
• *The Diary of Anne Frank* (1995) Macmillan, London.

Useful Contacts
Amsterdam Schiphol Airport, ☎ 0900 503 4050. For flight enquiries and arrivals information, ☎ 020 474 7747.
Central Medical and Dental Service, ☎ 0900 503 2042.
Emergencies, ☎ 06 11.
Police, ☎ 06 11.
Police Headquarters, ✉117 Elandsgracht, ☎ 020 559 9111.

Reservations are made through a courtesy phone link and a built-in printer provides booking confirmation and details of how to reach the hotel.

Accommodation in the Randstad Towns: Places to stay in The Hague, Rotterdam, or their smaller neighbours are available, though the range is generally not as wide as in Amsterdam. Really cheap budget accommodation at the one- or two-star level, in particular, is not so readily available. Be aware, too, that hotel beds are at a premium throughout the tourist summer season in smaller towns, and that Rotterdam and The Hague are year-round business, conference and exhibition destinations, where hotel rooms generally command a high price. It is advisable to make your accommodation arrangements before leaving Amsterdam –

either through the VVV or NRC systems, or through one of the many tour agencies in Amsterdam.

Eating Out
The choice of restaurants in the city centre reflects Amsterdam's ethnic mix and its position in the heart of Europe, with Tex-Mex, Argentinian and Chilean restaurants, Greek tavernas, German beer-cellars, Italian pizzerias and Turkish, Spanish, and Portuguese eating places. There are also plenty of Middle Eastern (mainly Turkish and Lebanese) establishments as well as Far Eastern restaurants including Indonesian, Chinese and Japanese cuisine. Amsterdam cannot claim to be among Europe's cheaper dining cities, but for those on a budget there are plenty of snack bars selling local favourites like pickled herring as

well as imported snacks such as felafel, pizza and kebabs.

Eating out in the Randstad Towns:
The heart of each of the smaller Randstad Towns is the medieval market square, known as the Markt. These pretty squares are conveniently lined with cafés and restaurants, many of which offer outside tables in summer. You will also find basic fast-food outlets selling the usual Dutch snacks like meatballs, herring, burgers and french fries in and around each station concourse. Throughout Amsterdam and the Netherlands, look out for the soup tureen logo of **Stichting Neerlands Dis**, an association of hotels which offer authentic Dutch regional dishes with a three-course meal at a very reasonable price. Look out too for restaurants taking part in the Netherlands Board

of Tourism's Tourist Menu scheme, which serve a three-course dinner offering value for money.

Transport
Air: Travelling by air within a country as small as the Netherlands is pointless. Distances are so short that rail travel is virtually always more convenient. **KLM CityHopper**, ☎ 020 474 7747, operates flights between Amsterdam and Groningen in the north of the country and also Maastricht in the south.

Rail and Bus: Trains leave frequently from Amsterdam Centraal Station, ✉ Stationsplein (☺ open Mon–Fri 07:00–19:00, weekends 08:00–19:00, ☎ 0900 92 92) for all the Randstad towns. Long-haul bus routes are also operated by Netherlands Railways; route and schedule information is available on the same number.

Road: Car rental is not advised for exploring Dutch cities as distances are very short, parking is always a problem, and fines for illegal parking are heavy. However, for those wishing to explore further afield, car rental is available in the city centre and at Schiphol Airport.

Avis:
✉ 380 Nassaukade
☎ 020 683 6061;
✉ Hogehilweg 7
☎ 020 564 1611.

Europcar:
✉ 51/53 Overtoom
☎ 020 683 2123;
✉ Schiphol
☎ 020 316 4190.

Hertz:
✉ 333 Overtoom
☎ 020 612 2441;
✉ Schiphol
☎ 020 610 5416.

Driving licenses issued by other EU countries are valid. Non-EU visitors need an International Driving Licence, obtainable in the Netherlands or before you leave. When renting a car, full collision damage waiver and liability insurance is highly recommended. Drive on the right-hand side of the road and observe the speed limits of 50 kph (30 mph) in towns, 80 kph (50 mph) on main roads and 120 kph (74 mph) on motorways. Rear-seat and front-seat passengers and drivers must all wear seatbelts.

In an **emergency**, contact the Dutch motoring association ANWB from motorway emergency telephones or ☎ 06 08 88.

Maps and motoring guides are available from all the VVV tourist offices.

On foot: Many of Amsterdam's streets are pedestrianized, and all have separate cycle lanes. On non-pedestrianized streets, pedestrians should be especially alert for trams, which have right of way over everything and everybody, and cyclists. Both move silently, and often the first warning that they are almost upon you is the sound of an irritated ringing bell.

Business Hours

Banks and public offices open Mon–Fri 09:00–16:00. Shops open Mon–Sat 08:30–17:30. Some shops stay open late on Friday evening – until 21:00.

Time Difference

GMT +1 hour.

Communications

The area dialling code for Amsterdam is 020 for calls from within the Netherlands and 00 31 20 for calls from abroad.

General Post Office, ✉ 250–256 Singel ☎ 020 556 3311 🕒 Mon–Fri 09:00–18:00, Sat 10:00–13:30.

Telecenter PTT Telecom (telephone, fax, telex and telegram services), ✉ 48 Raadhuisstraat ☎/📠 020 626 3871 🕒 daily 08:00–02:00.

AT&T Netherlands, ✉ 733 Strawinsky-laan, ☎ 020 570 2100.

AT&T USA direct service, ☎ 06 022 9111.

Electricity

Electrical supply is standard mainland European 220V AC. Plugs have two round pins.

Weights and Measures

The Netherlands uses the metric system.

Health Precautions

No special health precautions are required in the Netherlands.

Health Services

Private and public medical services are readily available and are of a high standard. European Union residents holding an E111 certificate – available from your doctor or health department before departure – are entitled to free medical treatment.

Central Medical and Dental Service, ☎ 0900 503 2042.

Personal Safety

Amsterdam has a relatively low rate of violent crime but non-violent thefts from the cars, hotel rooms and pockets of unwary tourists are not uncommon. Follow the normal precautions. Police advice is to leave your valuables and money in the safe of your hotel, and to carry no more money on you than you need.

Emergencies

General emergencies (police, fire brigade, ambulance): ☎ 06 11.
Police: ☎ 06 11.
Police Headquarters: ✉ 117 Elandsgracht ☎ 020 559 9111.

Etiquette

There are no special requirements or unusual local conventions.

Language

English is spoken fluently by almost everyone throughout Amsterdam and the Netherlands; English-language tourist information, maps, and restaurant menus are widely available. Though most of the letters of the alphabet are pronounced the same in Dutch as in English, there are several traps for the unwary. Vowels are lengthened, logically enough, by doubling them (as in centraal or nationaal), but some vowel combinations have unexpected results: *ui*, *ei* and *ij* are all pronounced to rhyme with 'eye'. In consonant combinations such as *kn*, each letter is pronounced as a separate sound. In Dutch, *v* is pronounced like an English *f* and *w* like an English *v*. The letter *g*, as well as the combinations *gh* and *ch* are pronounced like the *ch* in the Scots 'loch' (which is why foreigners find it so hard to get their lips round Van Gogh). *J* is pronounced like *y* is in 'yesterday'.

Useful Words and Phrases

Yes • *Ja*
No • *Nee*
Please • *Astublieft*
Thank you • *Dank u, bedankt*
Sorry • *Pardon*
Hello • *Dag*
Goodbye • *Tot ziens*
Good night • *Welterusten*
Left • *Links*
Right • *Rechts*
When • *Waneer*
Where • *Waar*
How far to ... • *Hoe vaar naar...*
Station • *Station*
Hotel • *Hotel*
Guesthouse • *Pension*
Chemist • *Apotiek*
Post office • *Postkantoor*
Hospital • *Zeekenhuis*
Doctor • *Dokter*
Bank • *Bank*
Toilet • *Toeleten*
I come from ... • *Ik kom uit ...*
Where is ...? • *Waar is ...?*
1 • *een*
2 • *twee*
3 • *drie*
4 • *vier*
5 • *vijf*
10 • *tien*
50 • *vijftig*
100 • *honderd*
200 • *tweehonderd*
1000 • *duizend*
Monday • *Maandag*
Tuesday • *Dinsdag*
Wednesday • *Woensdag*
Thursday • *Donderdag*
Friday • *Vrijdag*
Saturday • *Zaterdag*
Sunday • *Zondag*

INDEX OF SIGHTS

Name	Page	Map
Albert Cuypstraat Market	32	B–E4
Allard Pierson Archaeological Museum	35	A–D4
Amsterdams Historisch Museum	19	A–D4
Anne Frank Huis	25	A–B2
Antiquemarkt de Looier	53	A–A4
Artis Zoo and Museum	48	B–G3
Begijnhof	20	A–C4
Bijbels Museum	38	A–B4
Blauwe Theehuis	40	B–C4
Bloemenmarkt	52	A–D5
Boerenmarkt	52	A–C1
Casa Rosso Erotic Theatre	42	A–E2
Concertgebouw	72	B–D4
De Walletjes	42	A–E2
Delft	79	G
Electric Ladyland	49	A–B2
Erotic Museum	43	A–E2
Geels & Co, Koffie en Theemuseum	36	A–E3
Gouda	83	J
Haarlem	82	C
Hash Marijuana Hemp Museum	35	A–E3
Heineken Brewery Museum	33	B–E4
Het Rembrandthuis	22	A–F4
Holland Casino	70	A–B6
Hollandsche Schouwburg	37	B–F3
Hortus Botanicus Amsterdam	24	B–F3
Joods Historisch Museum	23	A–F5
Koninklijk Paleis	17	A–D3
Leiden	81	D
Madame Tussaud Scenerama	49	A–D3
Magna Plaza	51	A–D2
Martin Luther Kingpark	40	B–F6
Melkweg	71	A–A5
Museum Amstelkring	31	A–E2
Museumwerf 't Kromhout	37	B–G2
Muziektheater	73	A–F4
Nationaal Vakbondsmuseum	36	B–F2
Nederlands Filmmuseum	38	B–C3
New Metropolis Science and Technology Centre	49	B–G2
Nieuwe Kerk	30	A–D2
Nieuwmarkt	52	A–E3
Noorderkerk	34	A–C1
Oude Kerk	21	A–E2
Portuguese Synagogue	45	A–F4
Postzegelmarkt	53	A–C3
Rijksmuseum	14	B–D3
Rijksmuseum Vincent van Gogh	16	B–D4
Rommelmarkt	53	A–B4
Rotterdam	80	H
Scheepvaart Museum	29	B–G2
Six Collection	26	A–E5
Spui Kunstmarkt	51	A–C4
St Nicolaas Kerk	34	A–F2
Stadsschouwburg	74	A–B6
Stedelijk Museum	18	B–D4
The Hague	78	F
Theatermuseum	38	A–C2
Theatre Carré	71	A–F6
Thorbeckeplein Art Market	52	A–E5
Tropenmuseum	35	B–G3
Utrecht	82	E
Van Loon Museum	36	A–D6
Versetzmuseum	38	B–G2
Vondelpark	39	B–C4
Waterlooplein	51	A–F4
Westerkerk	28	A–B2
Willet Holthuysen Museum	27	A–E5
Woonbootmuseum	38	A–B4
Zuiderkerk	34	A–E4

General Index

Page numbers given in **bold** type indicate photographs

A

accommodation 55–59, 87–88
Ajax Amsterdam 41
Albert Cuypstraat Market **32**
Allard Pierson Archaeological Museum 35
Amstel Hotel **54**
Amstel River 7
Amsterdams Historisch Museum **19**, 44
Anne Frank Huis **25**, 44
Antiquemarkt de Looier 53
Armamentarium, Delft 80
Artis Zoo and Museum 47, 48, **49**

B

beaches 41
Begijnhof **20**, 44
Begijnkerk 20
Beurs van Berlage **73**
Bijbels Museum 38
Binnenhof, Den Haag **12**, **78**
bird life 8
Blauwe Theehuis 40
Bloemenmarkt 40, 44, **52**
Boerenmarkt 52
Bol, Ferdinand 15, 36
Bonaparte, Louis **11**
Bonaparte, Napoleon 11
brown cafés 63, **65**
Brueghel, Jan the Elder 14
bulb fields **7**, **46**
business hours 90

C

canals **6**, 7, 47
Cannabis Connoisseurs Club **42**
Casa Rosso Erotic Theatre 42, **43**
Centraal Museum, Utrecht 83
Cezanne 18
cheese **60**, **83**
churches *see* places of worship
City Cinema 71
climate 7
COBRA movement 18
communications 90
Concertgebouw **72**, 74
conference centre *see* RAI Congresgebouw
consulates 87
currency *see* money
customs 85

D

De Gelder, Aert 15
De Houtman, Cornelis 10
De Stijl movement 18
De Walletjes 42, **75** (*see also* red light district)
Delft 46, **79**
Den Haag **12**, 46, **78**
Descartes 9
diamonds 50
Domkerk, Utrecht 82
Dritt Shul 23
Duke of Alva 9
Dutch East India Company 10, 24, 35, 36, 45

E

economy 12
Eel Riots 43
Electric Ladyland 49
electricity 90
embassies 87
emergencies 91
English Church *see* Begijnkerk
Erotic Museum 43
etiquette 91
Euromast, Rotterdam **80**, 81
Exposeum Goudse Kaaswaag, Gouda 83

F

Flinck, Govert 15
food and drink 60–63, 88–89
Frank, Anne 25
Frans Hals Museum, Haarlem 82

G

gambling 70
Gassan diamond factory 45
Gauguin 16
Geels & Co. Koffie en Theemuseum 36
geniever 62
geography 6
Gevangenpoort Museum, Den Haag 78
Gouda 61, **83**
government 6, 12
Great Synagogue 23
Grote Kerk, Den Haag 78

H

Haarlem **82**
Hals, Frans 14, 26, 82
Hash Marijuana Hemp Museum 35
health 85, 90
Heineken Brewery Museum **33**

General Index

Herengracht 7
Het Prinsenhof, Delft 79
Het Rembrandthuis **22**, 45
Het Schielandshuis, Rotterdam 81
history 8–11
Holland Casino 70
Hollandsche Schouwburg 37
Hortus Botanicus Amsterdam **24**, 47
hotels 55–59
houseboats 54

I
IJ River 6
IJsselmeer 6
Inquisition 8

J
Jewish Quarter 45
Joods Historisch Museum **23**, 45
Jordaan district 6

K
Keizersgracht 7
Keukenhof flower gardens 46
Kindermuseum 48
Kloveniers Burgwal 7
Koninklijk Paleis **17**, 44
Kunst RAI 72

L
Lange Voorhout Palace Museum, Den Haag 79
language 13, 86, 87, 91
Lastman, Pieter 15
Leiden **81**
Lipsius 9

M
Madame Tussaud Scenerama 49
Madame Tussaud's Wax Museum 49
Magna Plaza **50**, 51
Marken 46
Martin Luther Kingpark 40
Master of Alkmaar 14
Mauritshuis, Den Haag 78
Melkweg 71
Mesdag Museum, Den Haag 79
Molen De Valk, Leiden 81
Monet 16, 19
money 86–87
Montelbaanstoren **45**
Museumplein 36, 44
museums
    Allard Pierson Archaeological Museum 35
    Amsterdams Historisch Museum **19**, 44
    Anne Frank Huis **25**, 44
    Armamentarium, Delft 80
    Artis Zoo and Museum 47, 48, **49**
    Bijbels Museum 38
    Centraal Museum, Utrecht 83
    Erotic Museum 43
    Exposeum Goudse Kaaswaag, Gouda 83
    Frans Hals Museum, Haarlem 82
    Geels & Co. Koffie en Theemuseum 36

museums (cont.)
    Gevangenpoort Museum, Den Haag 78
    Hash Marijuana Hemp Museum 35
    Heineken Brewery Museum **33**
    Het Rembrandthuis **22**, 45
    Het Schielandshuis, Rotterdam 81
    Joods Historisch Museum **23**, 45
    Kindermuseum 48
    Koninklijk Paleis **17**, 44
    Lange Voorhout Palace Museum, Den Haag 79
    Madame Tussaud's Wax Museum 49
    Mauritshuis, Den Haag 78
    Mesdag Museum, Den Haag 79
    Museum Amstelkring **31**
    Museum Boymans-van Beuningen, Rotterdam 81
    Museum Bredius, Den Haag 78
    Museum Lambert van Meerten, Delft 80
    Museum Tetar van Elven, Delft 80
    Museum voor Volkenkunde, Rotterdam 81
    Museumwerf 't Kromhout 37
    Nationaal Vakbonds-museum **36**
    Nederlands Filmmuseum 38

museums (cont.)
Nederlands Spoor-
wegmuseum,
Utrecht 83
Open Air Maritime
Museum,
Rotterdam 80
Prince Hendrik
Maritime
Museum,
Rotterdam 80
Rijksmuseum **14,
15**, 44
Rijksmuseum van
Oudenheden,
Leiden 81
Rijksmuseum
Vincent van Gogh
16, 44
Scheepvaart
Museum **29**
Six Collection **26**
Stedelijk Museum
18
Stedelijk Museum
de Lakenhal,
Leiden 81
Stedelijk Museum
Het Catharina
Gasthuis, Gouda
83
Theatermuseum 38
Tropenmuseum **35**,
47, 48
Van Loon Museum
36, **37**
Versetzmuseum 38
Willet Holthuysen
Museum **27**
Woonbootmuseum
38
Zuidhollands
Verzetsmuseum,
Gouda 83
Muziektheater 73, 74

N
Nationaal Vakbonds-
museum **36**

Nationale Ballet 73
Nederlands
Filmmuseum 38
Nederlands
Spoorwegmuseum,
Utrecht 83
Neie Shul 23
Netherlands Maritime
Museum *see*
Scheepvaart
Museum
Nederlandse Opera 73
Netherlands
Philharmonic
Orchestra 74
New Metropolis
Science and
Technology Centre
49
Nieuwe Kerk **30**
Nieuwmarkt 52
Noorderkerk 34, 44
Noordermarkt 52

O
Obbene Shul 23
Old Side 6, 42
Ons Lieve Heer op de
Solder 31
Oosterdok **29**
Open Air Maritime
Museum,
Rotterdam 80
Oude Kerk **21**

P
Panorama Mesdag,
Den Haag 79
Pathe Tuschinski
Cinema 71
people 13, 76
Peperbrug 45
Picasso, Pablo 18
Pieterskerk, Utrecht
82
places of worship
Begijnkerk 20
Domkerk, Utrecht
82

places of worship
(cont.)
Dritt Shul 23
Great Synagogue
23
Grote Kerk, Den
Haag 78
Neie Shul 23
Nieuwe Kerk **30**
Noorderkerk 34, 44
Obbene Shul 23
Ons Lieve Heer op
de Solder 31
Oude Kerk **21**
Pieterskerk, Utrecht
82
Portuguese
Synagogue 23, 45
Sint Bavo Kerk,
Haarlem **82**
Sint Janskerk,
Gouda 83
St Nicolaas Kerk
34
Westerkerk **28**, 44
Zuiderkerk **34**, 45
population 6
pornography 43
Portuguese Synagogue
23, 45
Postzegelmarkt 53
Prince Hendrik
Maritime Museum,
Rotterdam 80
Prince William of
Orange 9
Prinsengracht 7
public holidays 84

Q
Queen Beatrix 10, 12

R
RAI Congresgebouw
72
red light district 6, 42,
70 (*see also* De
Walletjes)
Reformation 8

Rembrandt *see* Van Rijn, Rembrandt
restaurants 64–69
Rijksmuseum **14**, **15**, 44
Rijksmuseum van Oudenheden, Leiden 81
Rijksmuseum Vincent van Gogh **16**, 44
rivers
  Amstel 7, **54**
  IJ 6
Rommelmarkt 53
Ronde Blauwe Theehuis *see* Blauwe Theehuis
Rotterdam **80**
Royal Concertgebouw Orchestra 72
Royal Palace *see* Koninklijk Paleis

S
Saenredam, Pieter 26
safety 91
Scheepvaart Museum **29**
Scheveningen 41, 46
Singel 7
Sint Bavo Kerk, Haarlem **82**
Sint Janskerk, Gouda 83
Six Collection **26**
Six, Jan **26**
Spinoza 9
Spui 44, 51–52
Spui Boekenmarkt 52
Spui Kunstmarkt 51

St Nicolaas Kerk 34
Stadhuis, Gouda 83
Stadhuis, Leiden **81**
Stadsschouwburg 74
Stedelijk Museum **18**
Stedelijk Museum de Lakenhal, Leiden 81
Stedelijk Museum Het Catharina Gasthuis, Gouda 83
Steen, Jan 14
Stopera *see* Muziektheater

T
The Hague *see* Den Haag
Theatermuseum 38
Theatre Carré 71
Thorbeckeplein Art Market 52
Tintoretto **14**
Toulouse-Lautrec 16
tourist information 84
tours 46, 47
Trade Union Museum *see* Nationaal Vakbondsmuseum
transport 84, 85–86, 89–90
Tropenmuseum **35**, **47**, 48
tulips 40

U
United East India Company *see* Dutch East India Company
Utrecht 82

V
Van Gogh, Vincent 16, 18, 44, 81
Van Loon Museum 36, **37**
Van Rijn, Rembrandt 9, 15, 21, 22, 26, 28, 36, 45, 81
Van Ruisdael, Jacob 14, 26
Van Vondel, Joost 39, **40**
Vermeer, Jan 9, 14, 15
Versetzmuseum 38
VOC *see* Dutch East India Company
Volendam 46
Vondelpark **39**

W
Waag 45
Walletjes *see* De Walletjes
Waterlooplein 45, **51**
Westerkerk **28**, 44
Willet Holthuysen Museum **27**
William the Silent *see* Prince William of Orange
Woonbootmuseum 38

Z
Zaanse Schans 46
Zandvoort 41
Zuiderkerk **34**, 45
Zuidhollands Verzetsmuseum, Gouda 83